COME WALK THE WORLD

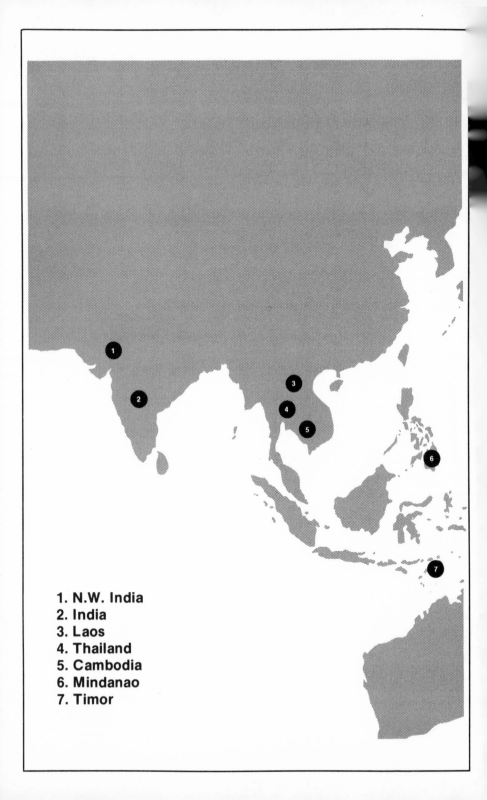

1. N.W. India
2. India
3. Laos
4. Thailand
5. Cambodia
6. Mindanao
7. Timor

Personal experiences
of hurt and hope

COME
WALK
THE
WORLD

by W. Stanley
Mooneyham

WORD BOOKS
PUBLISHER
4800 WEST WACO DRIVE
WACO, TEXAS
76703

Portions of the material included in this book have
previously appeared in World Vision Magazine.

Photo credits: Chapter 1, Eric Mooneyham; Chapter 2, W. Stanley
Mooneyham; Chapter 3, Eric Mooneyham; Chapter 4, Eric Mooneyham;
Chapter 5, Eric Mooneyham; Chapter 6, Robert Larson; Chapter 7, Eric
Mooneyham; Chapter 8, Eric Mooneyham; Chapter 9, Robert Larson;
Chapter 10, Eric Mooneyham; Chapter 11, W. Stanley Mooneyham;
Chapter 12, Eric Mooneyham.

ISBN 0-8499-0076-x
Library of Congress Catalog Card Number: 77-92471
Printed in the United States of America

Jacket and book design: Don Aylward

To
LaVerda
who agreed we should
share
the adventure

Contents

Preface

1. A Love Affair in Cambodia 15
2. By Mule Train to the Kachins 31
3. Famine . . . and One Man's Family 43
4. When God Came to Timor 53
5. The King of All Floods 67
6. Where Only Man Is Vile 77
7. A Green Thumb Grows in Kenya 89
8. The Angry Winds of Andhra 99
9. No Place Left to Run 111
10. God's Second Visit to Timor 123
11. The People Behind the Wire 135
12. God Is Still in Control 145

·

Preface

These vignettes from more than twenty years of international Christian ministry are partly reliving an experience for me, and partly written to help you get some personal, human, and warm glimpses into the "world" that to many of us is almost as unknowable as outer space.

I find that many people in the West feel estranged from the rest of the world. In spite of Dag Hammarskjöld's statement that "there are no distant places in the world anymore," the world still seems to us mysterious, removed, hard to understand. We measure it by our own frame of reference, and when it sometimes appears out of sync, we get frustrated. Why can't everyone be like us, we want to know? When they aren't, or when they act in an unfamiliar way, we are ready to pull back to our knowable and "safe" boundaries.

I think this partly accounts for our periodic national withdrawals into isolationism. Sadly, that syndrome also demonstrates itself in the church, and as a result the commitment to mission ebbs and flows.

I well remember my first trip outside the United States. Even as an adult, I experienced pangs of homesickness. That was twenty-one years and over two million miles ago. The world long ago ceased to be strange to me. Geographically, if not philosophically, it has become my home. It may sound hyperbolic and even a bit melodramatic, but I feel that John Wesley's words are literally true for me. The world *is* my parish.

To me it is now a familiar, friendly place. I experientially endorse Marshall McLuhan's concept of the "global village." When I travel outside my homeland—which I still do for about six months each year—I never feel like a stranger in a strange land. Whether among the former headhunters of Nagaland, the primitive Masai of East Africa, or the sophisticated, delightfully humorous Poles in Eastern Europe, I have the feeling of being with my family.

That is doubly true. In the general sense, we are members of the same human family because God "has made of one blood all nations of men for to dwell on all the face of the earth" (Acts 17:26). More specifically, I have a unique spiritual kinship with those who know Jesus Christ in saving faith. I have found these brothers and sisters everywhere. The attraction is mystical and magnetic.

A few years ago, two friends and I were visiting East Germany, seeing the landmarks in the life of Martin Luther. One stop was Wartburg Castle at Eisenach, where Frederick the Wise hid Luther from angry church authorities. It was here during this period of enforced isolation that Luther translated the Book of Romans into the common language.

The group of East Germans with whom we were going through the historic place were secularists, if not Marxists. They were more interested in the architecture, the tapestries, and the relics than in Luther's association with the castle. When we came to Luther's room, they moved on rather quickly. My friends and I stayed and asked our guide a thousand and one questions. She was an elderly lady and seemed delighted at our special interest.

After a while, she quietly asked, "Are you believers?"

When we told her we were, tears came to her eyes as she gripped our hands in warm fellowship. Then she used a rich metaphor:

"Oh, I knew you were because sparks just flew between us!"

I love that.

Because I know so many of God's choice servants in so many places in the world, I refuse to allow my view of the world to be politicized. After all, there were saints even in Caesar's household.

A Polish Christian said to me: "Why should we allow politicians to erect an 'iron curtain' between believers?"

Why indeed? Jesus didn't let politics keep him out of Samaria.

My life is infinitely richer because God has allowed me the privilege of walking his world. I hope that sharing these intimate and personal experiences will contribute something to your own life.

Centuries ago the Bishop of Hippo Regius in Numidia in Roman North Africa, better known as Saint Augustine, spoke a contemporary truth when he said, "the world is a great book, of which they who never stir from home read only a page." Well, maybe you can't "walk the world" as a physical experience. Never mind. You can still be a global person as you read, pray, and share globally

I once heard my colleague and beloved friend, Paul Rees, describe a walk as " a step repeated." I hope each chapter of this book will be for you a step forward into God's exciting world.

Come on. Let's take a walk together.

W. Stanley Mooneyham

COME WALK THE WORLD

Chapter 1

A Love Affair in Cambodia

My love affair with Cambodia began in 1970.

We were first introduced in 1968, and although I was bewitched by this demure little oriental maiden, one could not really say it was love at first sight.

Infatuation, maybe. But Cambodia took a little getting used to.

Like her sister, Laos, she was different from the rest of the family. I knew their cousins—Hong Kong, Singapore, Tokyo, Bangkok, Jakarta. Without exception, they were gaudy, brash, loud, and lusty. One just expected the less public relatives to be the same.

Then I met Phnom Penh. She was scarcely aware of my presence at first, but I was fascinated by her. If the rhythm of the rest of Asia was a frenzied rock-and-roll, Phnom Penh moved in waltz time.

After moving to the frantic beat of the rest of the continent, I found the calm and unhurried gait of Phnom Penh an immediate change of pace. And if you could break the hectic-and-hurry habit of Western living, you just might find yourself falling into the flow of things.

I did. Happily.

And the more I knew Cambodia, the more I loved her. Technically, I suppose one would say it was not

The war in Cambodia produced thousands of orphans and we were privileged to care for many of them. Now I weep for them and their beautiful country.

Cambodia I loved, but her people. Ah, the Khmer people. Gentle, shyly courteous, warmly hospitable, trusting, patient, naive, and unsophisticated. Collectively, Cambodia's seven million people were like an unspoiled country girl.

Maybe that's what was wrong. War catapulted them into the twentieth century which had no time or place for naive country girls. Cambodia was a babe in the woods. She had to grow up fast—learn to protect herself, find out who to trust, get an overnight education in international politics, and play diplomatic parlor games with potentially disastrous consequences.

It was more than one could expect from a country girl. And in five years, I saw her betrayed, terribly abused, and brutally raped.

She was the victim of her own innocence.

The experience sent me into deep depression for which I had to be medically treated. The depression is gone, but the pain is still inside. Maybe talking about it will help, for I firmly believe our romance—Cambodia's and mine—was divinely arranged.

When I knew her best in the early 1970s Cambodia was already aflame with the war which had engulfed Southeast Asia. Unprepared both physically and psychologically for this cruel assault on its land and life, the ancient kingdom of the Khmers tried to fight back. The futility of the whole thing was best demonstrated by the conscripted civilians I saw going off to war—after thirty days' training—riding on commandeered Pepsi–Cola trucks and wearing rubber sandals.

It was pathetic and ludicrous.

The Khmer kings had once been fierce warriors, ten centuries ago in the heyday of Angkor Wat. But Buddhism and a couple of centuries of French rule had helped pacify the people. The average Cambodian of the 1970s lived quietly, if not richly. His peasant life moved at a tranquil pace, like the Mekong and Tonle Sap rivers which meandered through the rice paddies.

War shattered it all. Villages were terrorized. Almost overnight Phnom Penh became a fetid, sprawling refugee camp. The call went out for humanitarian assistance, but hardly anyone responded. Cambodia was an unpopular cause, a political liability. Relief agencies stayed away in droves.

I saw it differently. It could be a spiritual opportunity for an agency that cared more about service than prestige. Up to that time, Protestant Christianity had fared rather poorly at the hands of both government and people. The people, satisfied with Buddhism, ignored the churches while the government persecuted them. Missionaries had been booted out, churches closed, pastors imprisoned, and the number of believers had bottomed out at around six hundred out of a population of seven million.

There wasn't much to be lost by trying.

Drew Sawin, the son of former missionaries to Vietnam, introduced me to Cambodia at war. He had lived in the land for a year, researching his university thesis. He had also tried to persuade Prince Norodom Sihanouk, Cambodia's head of state, to readmit the expelled missionaries. He knew people—and his friends became our friends.

These officials of a fledgling government showed us the battered land. The scenes of burned-out villages, overflowing hospitals, and festering refugee camps are still etched deeply in my memory. No one has spoken it better than General William Sherman: "War is hell."

A country which had almost nothing, needed everything. Larry Ward, then a vice-president of World Vision, reminded me that World Vision had a good supply of food supplements and medicines in our warehouse in Saigon. Remembering the apostolic generosity, "Such as I have, give I thee," we agreed to help.

That was no problem. Getting the stuff from Saigon to Phnom Penh over 150 treacherous and uncertain miles was something else. The road—grandly named Highway One—traversed the infamous area known as the "Parrot's Beak." The Viet Cong roamed freely throughout the area and at least half the route was subject to frequent ambush. Furthermore, the border between the two countries had been only recently opened by the simple expediency of cutting through coils of tangled barbed wire, but no immigration formalities had been established. It wasn't necessary. Civilians—especially foreign ones —simply weren't crossing the border.

It was, one could say, a high-risk venture—and not to be undertaken lightly.

I prayed for 20/20 foresight. It didn't come. I had no certainty we would make it. I only felt compelled to try. On Sunday night in Saigon I met with Larry, Drew, and Gordon Diehl (the other member of our foursome) to assure them they had total liberty to withdraw if any of them did not feel that same conviction. There was unanimous agreement—and we committed the mission to God in prayer.

At the dinner table that night in the World Vision guest house, a businessman from Singapore slipped a paper bag onto my lap under the table. Curious, I peeked inside. It was cold steel—a .45 caliber pistol with an extra clip! Thanking him for his thoughtfulness, I quickly handed it back. Not only had I never handled one in my life, but I couldn't quite see trying to insure a mission of total faith with a .45 pistol.

Early the next morning, Gordon and Larry climbed up into the big truck which was loaded with ten tons of tangible love. Drew and I took the Jeep Wagoneer, a gift to the Cambodian Red Cross.

Now there was no turning back. Never mind. God still seemed to be saying, "Go." In an effort to slow down my pulse, I tried to equate this feeling with a divine guarantee of safety. I couldn't. The only thing I knew for sure was that the purpose of God would be ultimately served by what we were doing. Nonetheless, I knew enough about the ways of God to understand that his purposes are sometimes better served by our dying than by our living.

I thought I could hear Queen Esther saying, "If I die, I die." I wondered if she, too, had been scared.

The words came back to me many times. I do not recall having a normal heartbeat all day. My heart pounded doubletime—especially on those lonely stretches of road where we saw no human beings, usually a sign of roadblock and ambush ahead.

The trip was as much a test of patience as of faith. We fumed at bureaucratic delays, malevolently contrived, it seemed, to stretch a five-hour trip to over two days. That would have necessitated spending one night among the mosquitoes and Viet Cong. Highway One is one of the few roads in the world along which Holiday Inns has not sold a franchise.

We blitzed the Vietnam/Cambodia border when a Vietnamese guard couldn't read our permits written in Khmer, and his Cambodian counterpart a hundred yards away insisted on getting approval from his colonel in Svay Rieng, an hour up the road. It wasn't that I was thumbing my nose at formalities. I just thought they had their priorities mixed up.

We detoured around a dozen dynamited bridges, fording shallow rivers and thanking God it was still the dry season. One bridge, not yet sabotaged, was guarded by a small ragtag group of men with rifles. As we approached, their peasant clothes were apparent—a sure sign, I thought, they belonged to the other side. We drove slowly, prepared to surrender. It turned out they were Cambodians who had been sent to the front without uniforms!

I experienced what one television commercial would call "total relief."

At the end of what seemed like the longest day of my life, packed with enough adventure to last a lifetime, we reached Phnom Penh just ahead of sundown. God had watched over us. Only in heaven will we know the full extent of his protection that day. It had not gone so well with eight members of two television crews who had planned to meet us at the border and cover the relief mission. They had all been killed the previous day in the Cambodian countryside.

Again I had the vague feeling that God was standing in the shadows, arranging something beyond my capacity to understand.

A public ceremony was held the next day in which we turned over the supplies to relief officials. When asked to say something, I used the occasion to speak of the love of God which had motivated us to serve suffering humanity. These Buddhist officials smiled and nodded approvingly. I spoke of the caring love of Jesus Christ. There was no resentment, even though it was the first time in Cambodia's history that Name had been spoken in a government ceremony.

We didn't hand out any tracts or distribute any Bibles. At that moment it would have been grossly insensitive. We had been moved to share with a suffering people at the time of their greatest need. We had done so in the name of Jesus. Anything else could come later.

For now, words had become flesh. That was enough. I have learned that love talked about can be

easily turned aside, but love demonstrated is irresist-
ible.

Little by little, the long-held hostility against
Christianity began to melt away. The government
welcomed back the missionaries. The Khmer Evangelical Church, so recently emerged from persecution,
formed its own relief and witness teams to work
among the refugees.

As love had opened the nation, so now it began to
open many individual hearts. The church leaders felt
it was God's time to begin a public declaration of the
gospel. At their invitation—and with the government's full approval—I agreed to conduct the first
public evangelistic campaign ever held in the country. We were given use of the Moha Srop Tonle Bassac auditorium, a 1500-seat, air-conditioned theatre
on the banks of the Tonle Sap River.

The campaign was a giant step of faith for the little
church. It was scheduled for three days to coincide
with the Cambodian New Year. The promotion had
announced there would be "Good News for the
Khmer People." About forty young people had been
recruited for a choir. Thirty people had been trained
as counselors.

Our expectations were limited by history. The result of more than fifty years of Protestant missions in
the country, spearheaded by the Christian and Missionary Alliance, was a handful of churches and less
than 1,000 believers. Cambodia had a reputation as
one of the most difficult mission fields in the world.

I was both exhilarated and scared as I walked to
the platform that first day with my interpreter, Son
Sonne, secretary of the national Bible Society. To my
mind, the gospel I had preached for twenty-five years
was about to be put to the most severe test of my
ministry.

Our first surprise that day was the crowd. Never in our wildest imagination were we prepared for the thousands who had to be turned away. Every seat was filled an hour before time, and thousands outside pushed and shoved to get in. Among them was a schoolteacher named Sin Soum, about whom we'll hear later. He was very angry that someone would announce "Good News for the Khmer People" and then not have enough seats for everyone.

Inside, the crowd, made up primarily of young men, was friendly. I told the oldest story in the world in the simplest way I knew, for they had never heard it before. I started with God and creation and ended forty-five minutes later with Calvary and the resurrection. The crowd never turned hostile, but scores walked out scoffing as I spoke of the virgin birth, the miracles of Jesus, and his resurrection. I remembered that " . . . the preaching of the cross is to them that perish foolishness."

On the plane from Bangkok to Phnom Penh I had stretched my faith to believe God for one hundred souls during the three days. Now I began to wish I had picked a lower number! What little confidence I had gained when I saw the overflow thousands was being fast eroded by the scoffers who were leaving. Everything I had learned earlier from the church leaders and missionaries had conditioned me for little or no response. They had told me how in the Khmer culture "to be different is to be wrong." The Buddhist religion was a part of the ancient cultural fabric and by asking people to change centuries of religious belief I was, to their minds, asking them to do wrong.

By the time I had finished the sermon, so sure was I of failure that I wished I could skip the invitation. But the gospel demands decision, so my preaching must conclude with a choice. I asked those to stand who would respond to a fourfold invitation—turn from their idols, repent of their sins, believe in the true and living God, and receive his Son, Jesus Christ, as Savior and Lord.

There were a few seconds of silence followed by a shuffling of feet. Then nearly half of those who remained—about 500 people—stood! Neither Son Sonne nor I felt any exhilaration, however. We simply thought they had misunderstood. So we went over the invitation again very carefully, then asked those who had misunderstood or were not serious in their response to be seated. Only a handful resumed their seats.

We were still incredulous. True, we had spoken God's Word, but we couldn't believe the miracle we were seeing. It was not possible. Such a thing had never happened before.

There had to be some other explanation. I struggled for ways to separate the "earnest seekers" from the "insincere"—categories I had established in my mind. I asked those in the latter group to sit down, and the "true believers" to come and stand at the front of the auditorium. Almost all came! Still I doubted. I kept remembering that in the Cambodian culture, to be different is to be wrong. I kept remembering that it had never happened before.

In a last desperate attempt to separate what I thought were the few grains of wheat from all the chaff, I asked those who were ready to give up all for Jesus to come and stand on the platform with me! Hundreds came. I could think of no more tests. Still perplexed—and emotionally drained—I could only ask the thirty counselors to take groups of up to twenty inquirers and instruct them from the Scriptures.

Only when I saw these groups gathered all over the auditorium, reading the Word of God and praying the sinner's prayer, did the truth of what was happening penetrate my unbelief. It was staggering! God had allowed me to be spectator to a great miracle, and my defeatist mentality had blinded me to it.

So devastating was that awareness when it hit me that I went over to a corner of the platform behind a curtain, sat down, and wept. I repented and asked God to forgive my unbelief.

The next day was another miracle. This time we had arranged a public address system outside so we could hold a service for the overflow crowd. The schoolteacher, Sin Soum, was back—again too late to get inside. He left upset again, but determined to come early enough the last day to get a seat.

The third day was a repeat of the first and second.

Sin Soum had a good seat in the balcony. I spoke on the second coming of Christ and paralleled his reign of peace with an ancient Cambodian legend. Sin Soum knew it well. The legend says that a great battle will take place where four rivers come together. It will happen at the end of the world. Cambodian tradition says it will be Phnom Penh, where the Tonle Sap and Bassac rivers join both legs of the mighty Mekong. According to the legend, the blood of battle will flow to the stomach of the elephant. At that time a god will come with scars in his hands, feet, and side. The legend describes this god as a *Sarmatre*—a god of peace. He will reign for 1,000 years with equality and justice.

I told the audience that the essential elements of the legend were true and that the name of the *Sarmatre* was Jesus. Sin Soum sat in the gallery and trembled. When the invitation to believe in Jesus Christ was given, Sin Soum said later, "I just leaped to my feet. I was the first one up."

He talked with a counselor, prayed, and hurried home to tell his wife, Kao.

"I've found the *Sarmatre*," he said. "I have peace!"

Kao just busied herself with the children and didn't say anything. Three months later she, too, became a Christian, however. She had seen the difference Jesus made in her husband's life.

No one knows how many actually became Christians during the crusade. It was impossible to know, but the number counseled was just under 2,000. However, the headline in our own magazine which said, "Suddenly the church has multiplied nearly three times" was certainly a bit of hyperbole. It couldn't have happened. The church simply was not ready to shepherd that many new believers.

There was no way the follow-up could be done adequately. The churches did not have enough people. Many of those counseled were refugees and had no permanent addresses. There were only four Protestant churches in the city and they were all small and virtually unknown. We learned later that numbers of the new converts went to the several French Roman Catholic churches—the only visible Christian presence in the city—and asked the priests what they should do now that they were followers of Jesus.

But no one could deny that a new power had been let loose in the land. It was God's breakthrough for which no man could take credit. Not only were we totally unprepared for it; we didn't even believe it when it happened.

For nearly half-a-century, the Cambodian Evangelical Church had been a church of the shadows. Its members had been beaten down, imprisoned, despised. Then almost overnight the situation changed. The name of Jesus could be spoken in public. Christians were no longer ashamed and afraid. They began to witness as never before. Bible study groups were formed all over the city and in refugee camps. Buddhist priests came to the homes of missionaries and asked about Jesus.

The Rev. Chau Uth, president of the church, told me: "We feel Phnom Penh has been shaken, turned upside down. Before, we were a hidden people, but now we are visible."

"I wouldn't believe this unless I had seen it with my own eyes," said Minh Tien Voan, an engineering graduate of the University of Georgia who became a Christian while a student in the United States. "One time I tried to get into the meeting and a young man standing there wouldn't let go of me. I thought he wanted to get inside, but I told him there were no more seats. He insisted he didn't want to go in; he just wanted to become a Christian. So I led him to Christ right there on the steps."

After the first meeting, I saw Voan, who was later to become deputy director of World Vision's programs in Cambodia, counseling two men on the steps. I thought he was introducing them to Jesus, but later he told me they had already been counseled as new believers. They had come to him asking if they could lead others to Christ, so he had been giving them an abbreviated counseling course!

I was beginning to get a glimpse of why God had first brought me to Cambodia. And why he had allowed us to drive safely from Saigon to Phnom Penh. As always, God had a plan and we were being permitted to share in it.

Six months later I was invited by church leaders to return to Cambodia for a second campaign. This time the Anglican archbishop of Sydney, Dr. Marcus Loane, agreed to join the team and lead the morning Bible studies. The response this time was like the first, except now a larger, more vigorous and spiritually alive church had been praying, witnessing, and working. And they were ready for the follow-up of inquirers.

God did more miracles. Several government officials responded to the message of Christ. Merle Graven, a missionary with the Christian and Missionary Alliance, saw one such man stand for whom he had been praying for fifteen years. Merle counseled the official, who asked Christ to change his life.

The president of the Supreme Court of Cambodia, Men Ny Borinn, asked to see me privately. He told me he had been a secret believer ever since someone had given him a New Testament many years before. He had never publicly declared his faith, but he wanted to do so now.

"I feel like I have become a torch," he said, "and I want to go around lighting candles."

Now six months later, Sin Soum was a member of the crusade planning committee. He had become a lay leader and he and Kao had discovered their own ministry. Outside the city was a large refugee settlement called "new Phnom Penh." It was Kao who first wanted to go. They counted the cost. Kao would have to walk fifteen minutes to the nearest well. Shopping was a half-day's journey. Soum would have to build some kind of shelter in which they could live.

But they felt a call.

With missionary zeal, Soum and Kao and their six children set out. Their first shelter was a little palm branch hut. Then Soum built a small wooden house next to the hut. As the family shared their faith with others, soon the little house was packed every night with people coming to study the Bible. Each Sunday the family moved out and Soum dedicated the building to the service of the Lord.

In six months, thirty people had become followers of Jesus. In three years, Soum was leading a congregation numbering over 1,000! Virtually all of them were his spiritual children or grandchildren. That group of believers was only one of the twenty-eight congregations—with some 10,000 in the worshiping community—which dotted Phnom Penh at the end.

When I last saw Sin Soum just about a month before Phnom Penh fell to the communists, he was still wearing the sign of the fish on the lapel of his cheap cotton shirt. He had adopted it shortly after his conversion. I don't know if then he understood the first century significance of it—that it was a secret sign among the persecuted and hunted followers of "the Way."

But the symbol may have been strangely prophetic, for the church in Cambodia today is underground. Perhaps secret signs are needed. Although I have heard nothing directly from Sin Soum since the land I love went behind a sad curtain of silence, I have a strong feeling I heard about him indirectly.

After his conversion, Soum told a colleague of mine that he had always wanted to be a leader, but he had never desired power. He explained: "As a boy I wanted to help people find a good way, a way of goodness."

Not long ago when I inquired of some Cambodian refugees who had escaped to Thailand regarding any knowledge they had of Christians, one told me he had heard about a very bold witness for Jesus in the area around Siem Reap, which happens to be where Sin Soum was originally from before the war drove him to Phnom Penh. This particular Christian, I was told, has become something of a legend because of his boldness and his leadership.

My heart leaped when I heard that! It must be Sin Soum, my son in the faith. As promised in the Bible, God is giving him the desires of his heart.

I hope somehow the Lord helped this wonderful man hear what I told him under my breath: "Keep going, dear brother, keep going. Remember, the saints overcame the enemy by 'the blood of the Lamb, and by the word of their testimony and they loved not their lives unto the death.' Be faithful and God will give you a crown of life. I love you and stand with you."

Then I knew that's what my love affair with Cambodia is all about—heroes and heroines for Jesus, like Sin Soum, Minh Tien Voan, Son Sonne, and all the others of whom this world is not worthy.

Chapter 2

By Mule Train to the Kachins

I felt so much at home as I sat around the campfire with my Kachin friends that I had to remind myself I was surrounded by some of the most famous—and most feared—guerilla fighters in the world.

Every time I am with tribal peoples anywhere in the world, especially in the mountain ranges of Asia, I feel this strange affinity with them. It is almost as if I were with my family. If I believed in reincarnation— which I obviously don't—I suppose I would say I was a tribal member in one of my previous existences.

Anyhow, I felt no apprehension—only a family closeness—as I sat with these youthful guerillas. As the reflection of the fire played across their bronzed features, I remembered what I had learned earlier about these beautiful people.

The Kachins (pronounced Ka-*chin*), numbering about 500,000, are a mountain tribespeople living in the north of Burma. If you count all the tribal cousins in the general area, the population is estimated at about two million. Animistic in background, they have been so open to the gospel that some of the groups are now more than 80 percent Christian.

Politically, the landlocked Kachin homeland is a

Kachin rebels on the tortuous mountain trail between northern Thailand and their home villages in Burma. The trip takes three months if there are no battles to be fought.

part of the Union of Burma, but it is a tie despised and vigorously contested by many of the Kachins who feel no kinship with Burma. They want an independent Kachin state and have formed themselves into a group known as the Kachin Independence Organization to push for political separation from Burma.

The military wing of this group is known as the Kachin Independence Army, and it was elements of this rebel force with whom I sat around the campfire.

Kachinland is a land of towering mountains and deep valleys, with peaks on the northern frontier reaching over 15,000 feet, creating spectacular scenery. Across those peaks on one side is China and on the other side, India. It is a little-known area, having lost its strategic value to the rest of the world after World War II.

Today it is known primarily to the outside world as being part of the "golden triangle," the mountainous areas of Laos, Burma, and Thailand where the best opium in the world is grown and where the growing of it is a way of life. The finest Burmese jade also comes from the Kachin area, but hardly anyone knows that.

Interestingly—and incongruously—it was opium that first introduced me to the Kachins.

At this point, a little political and geographical background will be helpful.

Because of its location at the center of Southeast Asia and because it allowed relative freedom of movement, Thailand in the early 1970s was filled with political intrigue. The jungles and vast mountain ranges of north Thailand were ideal places for the political crosscurrents of Asia to touch each other. For the most part, the Thai government established a *quid pro quo* relationship with the rebel forces who maintained hidden bases there. Although each group had its own particular priorities, the thing which made a tenuous togetherness possible was that they were all anti-communist. This stance also suited the military government of Thailand.

In one way or another, most of them were also involved in the opium traffic. It was inevitable since they controlled the back trails over which it moved. The Kachins and Shans from Burma grew the poppies, as did the Yao and Meo from Laos and other tribal cousins from Thailand itself.

The middlemen were the ragtag remnants of Chiang Kai-shek's Kuomintang army from south China which had settled in Thailand lock, stock, and rifles when Mao defeated Chiang. They bought the gummy raw opium and arranged for processing it into heroin. After twenty-five years, they still maintained an army and secret bases, but not with any thought of reentering China. They were there for the protection of the opium trade.

At the top of the drug hierarchy were a few wealthy Thai/Chinese in the northern cities of Chiang Mai and Chiang Rai who reduced the black gum to white powder and marketed it to countries all over the world.

It was a vicious and brutal business. Sometimes it was hard to tell where dealing in opium left off and fighting for freedom began. Both activities supported one of the area's major industries, arms-smuggling.

When General Zau Seng, commander of the Kachin Independence Army, sent word that he would like to see me I wasn't sure how he fit into this witches' brew. He had learned about our Christian humanitarian work through some missionary contacts. Those same contacts had assured me of his Christian faith, his integrity, and his desire to get his people out of the opium business.

Until now it has been impossible to reveal his name or tell this story because it would have added to the danger in which he constantly lived. However, in August, 1975, he was assassinated on the streets of Chiang Mai, presumably by other Burmese political elements.

When we met in late 1971, it was in the utmost secrecy. I was deeply touched by the humility and gentleness of this renowned and feared guerilla warrior. He spoke to me of his faith in Jesus Christ, of the deep yearnings of the Kachin people for independence from Burmese control, of his disappointment that the Western nations—especially the United States—had let down their former allies.

As a young man, Zau Seng himself had served with American forces against the Japanese in Burma. The Kachins had gained international fame during World War II as they fought with the Allies to open the Burma Road to the back door of China. Many of them risked their lives and some died to protect Americans shot down by the Japanese while flying "the Hump."

The bravery and sacrifice of the Kachins was immortalized in Tom Chamales' novel, *Never So Few*, which was made into a motion picture.

Now many of the Kachins feel disenfranchised by the subsequent political settlements, and they feel abandoned by the rest of the world. If they could vote on it, it seems certain that a majority would elect to withdraw from the Union of Burma. They want neither the socialist government nor the Buddhist religion of the Burmese.

On the other side, Zau Seng told me, their land was being swallowed up by the Chinese communists. This was confirmed by a story in the *Bangkok Standard Magazine* which reported, "Red Chinese troops, operating in large numbers inside a neighboring state for the first time since Tibet and Korea, have quietly taken control of much of northeast Burma in recent months."

For many of the Kachins it has been an unbearable vise and not a few have chosen to resist. On the south they face government troops determined to put down the rebellion, while on the same front armed elements of the Burmese Communist Party (Red Flag) also fight against the Kachins in alliance with the Chinese. On the north they face at least four Chinese divisions moving across their land, and the brave Kachins wonder if they will survive.

They remember Tibet and Korea.

General Zau Seng also wanted to talk about the opium trade. He told me most of the Kachin people grow the poppies because opium is an easy cash crop. Even though the tax on the opium derived from the poppies enables the Kachin Independence Organization to operate, he wanted to find some other way for the people to survive. Although most of those who grow it do not use opium as a narcotic, as a Christian the general wanted to stop the traffic from Kachinland. He knew the heroin derivative ended up in the veins of Western young people and this bothered him.

He asked me if I would talk to President Nixon and see if the United States government would help the Kachin people financially until they could find alternative means of income. It would take three to five years, but he would give his word that the opium growing would stop. One more thing, he said. Twenty-five tons of raw opium was on its way down the "opium trail" from the mountains. Was there some way the U.S. government could buy it either for medicinal use by pharmaceutical houses or simply to destroy it? I knew from reading the Bangkok press that we had already done the latter in at least one instance.

Zau Seng did not want this load to go to the middlemen and the merchants.

I could tell him only that I would try. It was a new field for me. I am an evangelist, not a diplomat. I didn't even know where to start.

Back home I made contact in Washington. It took a day just to find out to whom I should talk. It was my first real encounter with the government bureaucracy, and it was worse than I imagined. The appropriate officials in the narcotics suppression program listened to my story. Through their own sources they already knew the basics, so they did not doubt what I was telling them even though I was just an ordinary citizen with no official standing.

However, they told me the whole drug bureaucracy was under reorganization and it would take time for them to give me an answer. I waited—hopeful. I remembered that President Nixon had said drug eradication was a priority program. Zau Seng waited. When the answer finally came, it was negative.

No reason was given and I didn't try to guess. I assumed that politics or something else had been elevated to a high priority. The general was keenly disappointed. He told me I had been his last hope.

I don't know what happened to the twenty-five tons of heroin. I assume it was ultimately sold to the middlemen and the merchants.

Zau Seng was no stranger to disappointment. The Kachins have no friends in the international news media or at the United Nations. There is no one to tell their story to the rest of the world. The missionaries, who had provided their link with the outside world, were forced to leave in 1966 because the Burmese government felt they were a threat to the political stability.

Maybe it was because they were so alone that I accepted Zau Seng's invitation to visit the Kachin jungle training camp on the Thailand/Burma border and meet some of their young people.

After flying from Bangkok to Chiang Mai, I was called on at my hotel in the evening and told to be ready early the next morning. A Land Rover would pick me up at 6 A.M. We drove in a northwesterly direction for about three hours, finally stopping at a remote village which turned out to be settled by some of those remnants from the Kuomintang army. The Kachins and the Chinese have an "arrangement."

We would go the rest of the way, I was told, on mules. There were no roads to the camp. The mules were brought out of a secluded stable at the edge of the village. They were small—much smaller than those which used to pull our plows across the cotton fields in Mississippi. I wondered out loud if the one assigned to me could carry my six-foot-two-inch frame.

I need not have worried. The mule fared far better than I did! We climbed winding and precipitous trails to an elevation of over 5,000 feet. The rainy season was over, but lingering mud still slowed our rate of ascent. At times I looked straight down the face of a precipice as the sure-footed mule picked her way around the mud and over the rocks. At other times I just closed my eyes and held on.

The three-hour ride seemed like thirty. As we moved up the mountain, we passed several guard outposts. Finally, we arrived at the crest. Word of our coming had already preceded our arrival as the outposts had sent runners ahead. Since I was the first outsider ever to visit the Kachins here, they made the occasion an auspicious one.

It was not quite like riding in a ticker-tape parade down Fifth Avenue, but I enjoyed it more. As we approached Camp Peace, I dismounted—not regretfully—and walked under the simple evergreen arch which had been erected to mark the entrance. A "band" consisting of three drums and several bamboo flutes introduced me to this remote hiding place. The camp had been carved out of virgin land on the mountain top.

I came as a Christian brother and was so received.

Not long after I arrived, those who were not on duty gathered in the little thatched chapel for a worship service at which I was asked to speak. About five minutes into my sermon, I saw a guard run into the chapel and say something to one of the officers. I was told it would be necessary to interrupt the service temporarily since the Thai immigration police were on their way to the camp.

I was whisked away to a small building and hidden among rolls of woven bamboo for about half-an-hour until a routine check was made. Apparently someone had seen a six-foot-two-inch white man riding a donkey up the trail and had reported the strange incident to the immigration authorities!

No problem—it was a part of the *quid pro quo.*

The service resumed and I finished my sermon. A number of the soldiers stood in response to my invitation to receive Jesus Christ as personal Savior.

Around the campfire that night, the young people did folk dances, sang hymns, offered prayers, and shared testimonies of their faith and God's deliverance. One young man showed me a scar on his chest and told me that a Chinese bullet was still in his body.

There were stories of hope—and of despair.

In some areas of Kachinland, I was told, entire villages have fled to the jungle where they live under the most primitive conditions. People were dying from simple diseases that elementary medicine and diet could cure. Many are victims of a disease they call simply "swelling." It begins with a fever. The feet puff up, then the legs, then the whole body. Without treatment, death is only weeks away. But swelling is a condition that can be wiped out in a few days with a little vitamin B.

Food was in short supply in those areas as marauding troops adopted the "scorched earth" policy, burning the farmlands when the people fled to the jungles. The salt springs were burned down, making salt a precious commodity and contributing to the rising incidence of goiter. Clothes were in rags, and I was told that thread for weaving could not be imported. Medical facilities were almost non-existent.

In some places it seemed there was more liberty than in others, and the church thrived. Elsewhere the misery of physical suffering was made all the more acute by spiritual harrassment. Buddhism, the state religion, was taught to the children in schools. Soldiers shot up the churches and destroyed them. Kachin-language Bibles could not be officially imported.

The Chinese, on the other hand, turned the churches into lecture halls and the pulpits proclaimed the "gospel according to Mao." Pastors were persecuted when they would not support the communists. Families could not speak openly about Christ.

The Kachins—lovingly simple in their lack of Western sophistication—feel isolated and discouraged. Said one handsome young leader: "I keep telling my people that someday we will break through our isolation and people will listen to us. But we don't have the public relations Biafra had. We just have to keep hoping and praying for a miracle."

Perhaps my most touching moment was when a discouraged young major said, "It was the American missionaries who told us about Jesus and gave us our churches. Maybe they can't send us medicines, but why don't they send us Bibles?"

His naiveté prevented the question from sounding critical. As soon as possible after that, we had 10,000

New Testaments printed in the Kachin language by the Bible Society of Thailand and they were sent in a few hundred at a time with other supplies by mule-back.

It is extremely hazardous to get anything into Kachinland. Because of import restrictions imposed by the Burmese government, every item not on the approved list must go in by mules over those remote mountain trails. If the convoy is not attacked, which it frequently is, the trip takes two months.

(Later I learned that a convoy which left shortly after my visit to the camp was attacked several times and numbers of those with whom I had fellowshiped had been killed. My heart is still warm as I remember their simple faith, endless hope, and strong courage.)

I was extremely tired as I lay down on my bamboo bunk that night, but I felt no fear or apprehension. Young Kachin soldiers stood guard outside the little grass cottage as I switched off the flashlight and pulled four blankets over me to keep out the bone-chilling night wind.

I knew that not only was I among friends.

I was among brothers.

Chapter 3   Famine... and One Man's Family

The trip from Bombay to Ahmedabad to Singhali wasn't on our planned itinerary. Time, schedules, and other commitments simply made it impossible.

Period.

That's what I told my friend, the Rev. Raiji Rathod. This Methodist district superintendent had taken an all-night train ride to Bombay to urge us to visit his famine-stricken state of Gujarat in northwest India. I tried to be kind, but I felt I had to be firm. It just wasn't possible.

Quietly, he told us of widespread hunger, of Christian believers on the verge of starvation, of pastors who could not feed their families because their parishes had nothing left to share.

He wasn't insistent. He understood our problem. But his disappointment was obvious because—I found out later—we were his last hope. As we visited Bombay's slums and talked with Christian social workers that day, I couldn't get Raiji out of my mind. I knew he would leave within a few hours for another all-night ride on the train, his hope for help shattered. The thought bothered me, and I couldn't shake it loose.

In a small village in northwest India, I came face-to-face for the first time in my life with a Christian family on the edge of starvation. It challenged my theology.

43

Finally, in a compromise with myself I agreed that we would go the next day—*if* we could get seats on the plane to go and come in one day. But I was sure it couldn't be done at that late hour. Indian domestic airlines are frequently booked up days and weeks in advance.

Somehow I hadn't reckoned that this might be another one of God's significant detours. It was—and that's how it happened that we were at the airport at 5 A.M. the next day and, after an hour's flight, were bouncing along a dusty road toward one of Gujarat's hard-hit villages.

To get to Singhali you first fly to Ahmedabad, capital of India's Gujarat state, and then you start driving toward the Rann of Kutch—a no-man's land of drought, desert, and desolation. The two-hour drive confirmed everything Raiji and the newspapers had told us.

Raiji had not exaggerated when he said that the four-year drought had completely "broken the backs" of the villagers. Since the rains had failed again this year, many areas had been totally without food. Mr. A.P. Shinde, Union Minister of State for Food and Agriculture, said after a two-day visit to some of the drought-hit areas, "I did not find a single blade of grass during my tour of the interior."

I couldn't say the same because the last rain of a feeble monsoon had fallen shortly before we arrived, and some green shoots were coming out of the ground. Missionary pastor Gay Johnson assured me the sight was deceptive.

"This rice field we're standing in is a total loss," he said. "Even though it appears to be a bit green from last week's rain, it's a total loss."

Those words described just about everything around the village of Singhali. As we turned off the main road, we moved slowly over a rutted, wide dirt path that led toward the village. The further we went, the worse conditions appeared to be. Here and there only a few stalks of dying grain huddled together for comfort in the middle of patches of cracked, parched earth.

The village itself has stood at the end of this path for centuries.

The people have seen some good years and some bad ones. But since 1971 everything has been bad. The oldest villager can't remember anything worse since the "great famine" of 1900. That jibes with a newspaper article which reported the state in the grip of the worst drought in 75 years.

Affected in this one state are some 22 million people, and that is only 10 percent of the total number threatened throughout the country. I try to imagine 200 million people, but my mind boggles at the thought so I mentally come back to Singhali. Here are 2,500 people. That is a manageable number. I can relate to their plight.

The people welcome us warmly. It isn't often that strangers come to Singhali—particularly foreign strangers. But soon we are like friends. We are taken out of the heat to some shade, and scores of people gather around. Each would like to tell the story of his own disaster, but they allow the chief to speak for them.

Here is what he tells us: Only one-third of the people in the village own land. Each plot is small, having been subdivided to the sons for successive generations. In good years, however, each landowner can get up to 4,000 pounds of grain. This year the yield will be 50 to 60 pounds.

Normally, the other two-thirds who do not own land will work on surrounding farms as day laborers. This year there is no work for them.

The result: "My people are starving to death."

The words sound like hyperbole, but they are not. The chief speaks literally, without embellishment. He describes what it is like: "People will take whatever they can earn each day, maybe ten cents, and go and buy grain to make food. But there will be nothing for the next day. What they eat can scarcely be called a meal—a small millet cake or a piece of potato or eggplant."

Now there is a little work for a few people. The government has a project to deepen the dried-up water reservoir for the village. It is all done with hand labor for two reasons. First, there is no machinery available. Second, even if they had machinery, the people need the jobs. So the people dig with hoes and carry out the dirt in baskets on their heads. But apart from allowing the villagers to earn a few pennies, it means no immediate relief since the monsoon is already over.

"If it is bad now, what will it be like six months from now?" I ask. A man steps out from the crowd and echoes the question back to me: "Yes, how indeed will we be able to live?"

Missionary Gay Johnson gives a partial answer, but it is true for only a minority:

"Those who have land will mortgage it to get food grain for a year. This will give them perhaps one meal a day until the rains come. Then they will be in debt to the moneylender for the next five to ten years. If the rains fail again or if the people cannot get work, many of them will lose the two or three acres which they've had for generations and join the rest of the landless."

But what about those who are already landless and who have no jobs? This time the answer is more dramatic, for the pastor of the local church (there are twenty Christian families in the village) takes me over to one of his church families and says, "Ask them."

And that's how I was introduced to the effects of famine on one man's family. The experience was India, Gujarat and Singhali, but maybe the whole world, in microcosm.

His name is Gokal Walji Christie. (The "Christie" part, I am told, was added to indicate their new faith when the family became believers.) He is forty. His wife's name is Daruben. She is thirty. Both ages are approximate; they don't really know. There are four children; the oldest son is twelve and has been dumb since birth.

Gokal is a laborer, but he has had no work for more than six months. In normal times his family would have two meals a day. Now they are thankful when they have one.

Meal? Well, hardly. In the morning it's a cup of plain tea, no milk or sugar. In the afternoon (if there is enough for an afternoon meal), it's a small millet cake (*bajari*) with tea and maybe a raw onion or other vegetable. This is not enough calories for bare survival, much less for work.

"How does this affect you physically?" I inquire through the interpreter.

As with the answers to all my questions, this one is a matter-of-fact understatement: "We don't have enough strength because we don't have enough food. To work in the fields would not be possible even if there were jobs. I can barely work around the house. We are not in good health and our children also have the same difficulty. They don't grow healthy because they don't get sufficient food."

Stark. Honest. Devastating.

How does hunger affect their sleep?

"The children sleep whether they are hungry or

not. But we hold such feelings for them and we worry so for them, that we do not get enough sleep."

Do the children cry from hunger?

Tears fill the eyes of the mother and wet her cheeks as she says, "The children cry much of the time because they are hungry. It is hard for us not to weep with them."

It is a quiet, deep moment for us all. The mother continues, "For the next crop we will have to wait one more year. If God keeps us alive, we will remain alive. Otherwise we will go back to God, and that is what I expect."

For the first time in my life I am face-to-face with a fellow Christian who fully expects to die—soon—from starvation. David could say in the Psalms: "I have been young, and now am old; yet have I not seen the righteous forsaken, nor his seed begging bread" (Psalm 37:25). Now I can no longer share David's bold statement. The effect on my life then and later is incalculable. Never have I seen such serene faith and utter trust.

Never before have I talked with anyone who had to pray so literally, "Give us this day our daily bread."

"We don't envy any of the others who may have food," Daruben says. "Whatever God wants us to have today, he will give to us. We still depend upon him. There is no sharing of food in the village because everyone has the same difficulty. Some may have a little more than others, but that also is not enough."

Might life be better somewhere else? In one of the cities perhaps?

"Life is hard in the other villages as well," Daruben continues. She appears to be the spokesperson for the family. "We would like to move to a city, but we are told that there are no jobs there also. If we go to another place we will have no house for the children.

No, we have decided to stay in the village. If death comes, it is better to die among friends."

I talk about the children again. What hopes and aspirations do the parents have for them?

"We depend upon God for the children's future. Right now it is hard to make plans beyond survival."

I wonder how the children feel. Because the oldest can't speak, I turn to Julius, age seven. He is a shy lad, but with some gentle coaxing he begins to open up. He is one of the two children who go to school. The other is Naomi, age six.

What do you want to be, Julius, when you grow up? (A more accurate phrasing would be "if you grow up?" but honesty would be too brutal.)

His answer is bright and quick: "I would like to be a preacher, like my uncle."

Now comes a tough question. "Julius, if you could have anything in the world you want, what would you wish for?" It's an attempt to get down inside the mind and heart of a seven-year-old, to find out what he thinks about, what he dreams about. He doesn't answer right away. I don't know if he's thinking or reluctant to say, so I ask the question again.

When it comes, his answer devastates me: "For today, I would like a meal, and for the future, an education."

Spoken without emotion, straight, honest. No fantasizing. I decide that even at seven, when you have to live with "life vs. death" as the daily issue, there is no time for childhood dreams.

Again there is a hushed moment. I am moved by the simplicity of his wish, and all of a sudden it occurs to me, "That's a wish I can make come true—not as a good fairy, but as Christ's hands of love! That's exactly what World Vision's friends make possible all over the world—food and education."

Already my emotions are stirred, and the very

thought stirs such gratitude within me that I cannot hold back the tears. Quietly, through my friend, Raiji, I pass some money to the family with the promise of more to see them beyond this valley of the shadow of death through which they have been passing. Please tell them, I ask him, that through Christian friends who care, Julius will get an education.

There are other needs in the village to be met as well. I tell the pastor that we will send some money through the church so that they may help the entire village.

But water is both an immediate and long-range need. As we talk with the chief, one handsome, bearded Moslem comes out of the crowd and starts to talk to him as well. He is the owner of one of the few wells in Singhali still producing, but it is nearly dry and must be deepened. He isn't asking for help; he is stating a fact. One of the Christians tells me that this man, facing disaster himself, has continued to share the water in his well with Moslem and Christian alike.

When I tell him that his well would be one of the first projects in the village which we would help, he stands speechless. But the wells of water which form around his eyes speak more than words could ever say. With no attempt to wipe them dry, he just stands there and lets the tears flow.

He clutches my hand and will not let go. In his eyes I see the response to love—and his response is love also.

When we drove out of Singhali that afternoon, I had no doubt that this was one more unplanned "detour" which had been divinely arranged. And I was warmed and blessed by the thought that it must have been my Heavenly Father's response to the simple trust and prayers of one man's family.

Chapter 4   When God Came to Timor

I never doubted the miracles, even when I first heard about them in 1967. Oh, I confess the two rumored "resurrections" taxed my capacity to believe, especially since no one with whom I talked in Indonesia could personally confirm them. It was always, "I heard about. . . ."

But I didn't see the resurrections as being crucial to believing the rest. So when members of the evangelistic teams who had been on the island of Timor told me that God had accompanied the preaching of the gospel with signs and wonders, I was ready to believe.

Why should I doubt? Revival had come to many places in Indonesia. Believers were being added to the church, especially in Central and East Java, faster than they could be discipled. Stories were circulating around the world of five-and tenfold increases. I knew that physical manifestations have often accompanied movements of the Spirit of God.

I was in Indonesia to report on the revival. It had begun about 1964 when this fifth most populous nation in the world was in imminent danger of going communist. The country was spared that fate by a dramatic political reversal which many of my Indone-

Indonesian evangelist Petrus Octavianus and I share the joy and victory experienced by the people during a fetish-burning ceremony at the close of a crusade on the island of Timor.

sian friends still believe was God's divine intervention.

But the political upheaval had created horrendous social and economic problems for this island empire strategically located off the tip of Southeast Asia.

It was into this setting the Spirit of God wonderfully moved. The beginning of the revival is difficult to pinpoint because no one was looking for it. It may have started on the island of Java in 1964 with a Bible. A boy who had been attending a Christian school in Salatiga returned home to Central Java for the holidays that year with a New Testament in his pocket, a gift from the school. Religion seemed to have died out in his village of Communist sympathizers, but every evening the boy would read the stories about Jesus to his brothers and sisters. Soon some adults joined the group. Then friends and neighbors dropped in. All agreed they never had heard such beautiful stories.

Anxious to have the gospel explained, they sent a message to Salatiga asking for a preacher. When Pastor Soesilo came a group of 150 gathered to hear him, all of whom were baptized six months later. These told others and before long 12 adjacent villages had requested a preacher, and another 160 were baptized.

Although there were several unrelated movings of the Spirit almost simultaneously, that story from the Bible Society is as good as any to mark the beginning.

The people among whom God was moving were mostly animistic (spirit worshipers), but their animistic beliefs were covered with a veneer of Mohammedanism, and they were claimed as part of the Islamic fold. Even among the 10 percent of the population who were identified with the Christian faith, many still continued their idolatrous practices.

Although the church in the main was theologically orthodox, it was sadly deficient in spiritual life.

The Timorese Evangelical Church on the island of Timor was no different. It needed revival when it was visited by evangelistic teams from the Indonesian Bible Institute at Batu, East Java. Again, it is hard to mark the time and place of the exact beginning. One young man who was a member of a church in the interior town of Soe was convicted by the Holy Spirit of a fetish which he kept under his bed. It had been given to him by a *dukun,* or witch doctor, to help him run faster in sports. After one of the meetings, he went home, took the fetish, and threw it away.

He fully trusted Christ and asked the pastor if he could give a testimony at the next meeting. As he spoke and confessed his sin of witchcraft, conviction fell on the congregation and many repented. The meetings grew and the work of the Spirit spread.

Physical demonstrations of the presence and power of God began to be seen. There were healings. One church where revival had come glowed at night, as if it were on fire. A few people spoke in tongues.

It was these and other stories which I heard—and didn't doubt—in 1967. An Indonesian pastor explained it to me this way: "These people are very primitive. They've always lived in a spirit world, and they readily understand the conflict between God and evil spirits. With their childlike faith, miracles are no problem for them." Having met some of these new believers, I understood what my friend was saying. I did not question their word or his.

However, when I returned and wrote stories about the revival, I omitted reciting in detail the stories of the miracles. It was a deliberate omission, and there were three primary reasons:

First, since I had no way of personally verifying them, I did not want to be identified with retelling the stories. It was strictly a personal choice and in no way reflected disbelief. I just didn't want to be quoted as the authority for something I could not personally validate.

The other two reasons were more important. The second was that I was fearful these mind boggling stories would detract attention from the greater miracle of tens of thousands of animists and Muslims turning to Christ. I have been around long enough to see how much more excited we get over miracles in the physical realm than those which occur in the spiritual dimension.

My observation is that the Western mind—both Christian and pagan—is so jaded that it takes supernatural occurrences to arouse it. The Christians want miracles and signs; the pagans turn to witchcraft and the occult. Both are inordinately preoccupied with a desire for a cosmic breakthrough—divine or demonic —to stimulate their sated spirits.

I am not trying to start an argument with anyone who has had a charismatic experience. I respect every gift received from the Holy Spirit for use in the body of Christ. My concern is about our misplaced emphasis on the outward manifestation over the inner experience. I once asked Bishop Festo Kivengere from Uganda why the East African revival has continued for over forty-five years while most other revivals in history have tended to peak and wane after only a few years at the most.

His answer was that while the East African revival also had its physical manifestations in the early stages—including healing and tongues—the emphasis was never on the externals but always on the person of Jesus Christ. That priority, he said, has continued to the present time.

Jesus had a very important word to say to a generation that seeks for a sign.

My third reason for not reporting the stories of miracles was that the revival in Indonesia did not need these physical evidences to confirm its authenticity. What was happening in the churches was abundant proof that God was graciously visiting the country.

So I avoided the spectacular stories for what I considered valid spiritual reasons. But nearly five years after their actual happening, a young Timorese Christian visited this country and began to tell the stories—not only those which had been confirmed, but many which had not. His words fell into the eager vacuum of many earnest and honest people who longed to see the supernatural power of God demonstrated in their lives and churches.

Then began what I believe was a benevolent exploitation—honestly done, but with unhealthy results—by those who needed this sense of the spectacular. The stories were embellished with each telling, and new ones were added. The lines between past and present, reality and fantasy became blurred.

The stories were either enthralling or ludicrous, depending on your ability to believe. They told of resurrections from the dead, water turned into wine, playback from heaven of children's voices without benefit of tape recorder, and clothes that never got dirty. Expectably, they were recorded, transcribed, and published. *Like a Mighty Wind* sold a lot of copies. On the one hand it was praised uncritically, and on the other it was denounced vehemently. Some books were written refuting it, based on research and interviews in Timor.

Scores of people became confused.

What is the truth? Did miracles actually occur? Are they happening today? What part did they play in the revival?

Let me tell it as I know it and have experienced it. Undoubtedly miracles occurred. No one who really knows the situation disputes this. A missionary in Indonesia says: "We know that God has done miracles, although reports from responsible church people question some of the 'miracles' purportedly done by God."

There is no clash of faith and unbelief in that statement. It reflects a healthy attitude. Faith to believe in miracles does not preclude an inquiring mind. The Bible advises us to test the spirits. Whatever is truly of God will stand the test.

On the other hand, why should we stagger when God—who, if he is anything, is omnipotent and sovereign—sends miracles when and where he chooses to confirm his Word? In his book, *Miracles,* C. S. Lewis says, "The mind which asks for a nonmiraculous Christianity is a mind in process of relapsing from Christianity into mere 'religion.' "

In connection with the Indonesian awakening, it should be pointed out that the revival has never touched the whole country. Neither did it touch the whole church. Miracles were reported almost exclusively in the more animistic areas, and even there they began to drop away when the new converts got into the Scriptures. Having recently been to Timor for extended evangelistic meetings at the invitation of the Timorese Evangelical Church (see Chapter 10), I can tell you that miracles today are no more common there than any other part of the world.

But I also can tell you that the work of evangelism and renewal appears to be more solid now than in earlier days. A missionary wrote me: "It has long been a concern to many of us that the gracious work of God here has been commercialized. The deeper spiritual work of church renewal has been neglected in favor of the charismatic manifestations."

The big question everyone asks is, "Were people raised from the dead?" If you cannot believe it, you should not be troubled since there is not one medically confirmed case. Nothing is going to come unglued if your faith does not stretch that far. Mine doesn't. But if your faith does not stagger at the prospect, you can join the company of a few Timorese—and at least one missionary—who believe it happened. However, no one I have talked with endorses the book's claim that one man had been dead four days.

The one case to which they would give some credence involved the person having been "dead" for only a few hours. One man who knows the situation well from years of residence on Timor made this trenchant comment: "The people who comprised the witness teams around whose ministry the miracles occurred were wonderful people possessed, for the most part, with an innocent simplicity. If trained doctors are unable to agree on when a person is clinically dead, how should these people be expected to make that critical judgment?"

This same man feels that a great deal of charity must be exercised in evaluating the reports of the witness teams. All of those on the teams were spiritual infants. Almost all were young people. None were trained. Their knowledge of the Bible was elemental. Some were illiterate.

At one time more than 100 of these teams— numbering in personnel from 5 to 20—were scattered throughout the island. That these teams were greatly used of God no one will deny. Thousands found Christ. In two to three years the membership of the Timorese Evangelical Church doubled from 300,000 to 600,000.

Some signs accompanied the witness of the teams. Significantly, these usually occurred in connection with fetish-burning. Around these same fetishes in earlier days the witch doctors had done their own miracles. How appropriate that God would demonstrate his power as the fetishes were being burned!

But recognizing the faithful witness of these teams should not blind us to their human failures. There were excesses, including date-setting for the second coming of Christ. Also, there were exaggerations in the reports as successive teams tried to "keep up" with earlier ones regarding how God had worked. There was some immorality. And there was irrationality as for a while the "revelation" of specific sins in individuals preoccupied them and created serious tensions.

There is no need to overplay or underplay these things. They are there as part of the record, and that should shake no one's faith. Honesty contributes to credibility. The universe won't collapse if Christians admit to faults and failings. In the biblical record, the Holy Spirit never glosses over the frailties of even the holiest of saints.

As one Indonesian missionary says: "We certainly don't want to throw out the baby with the bath water, but people should not be misled by unbalanced reporting."

(1)With a few exceptions, the spectacular things reported in *Like a Mighty Wind* are certainly not happening in Indonesia today. The miracles which did occur happened mostly on the island of Timor and principally in the period of 1965–66. Some people still think that miracles are daily occurrences even now all over Indonesia. They are not. This does not mean, however, that the revival is over. The work of regeneration and renewal goes on, although not with the same intensity as in earlier years. If the "signs" are missing today, it means only that God sovereignly sent them for a particular purpose to a particular people at a particular time.

Again, C. S. Lewis has a helpful word here: "God does not shake miracles into Nature at random as if from a pepper-caster. They come on great occasions: they are found at the great ganglions of history—not of political or social history, but of that spiritual history which cannot be fully known by men."*

The revival in Indonesia was such a moment. Past experience teaches us that as the moment passes, so do the miracles. To try to reproduce them in another time and another context (or even in the same context) is an effort doomed to failure. And the failure, in addition to giving the enemies of God an occasion to scoff, could prove disastrous to the weak faith of some.

(2) *Like a Mighty Army* raises for many people the question: "Are charismatic spectaculars the norm for every revival?" Unfortunately, the book implies an affirmative answer.

I cannot accept that. Miracles are not served up on order. By their very definition they are the exception rather than the rule. It is important to know that miracles, tongues, and other charismatic expressions have not been the rule in the Indonesian revival. They have been the exception. Of the tens of thousands touched by the Spirit of God on Timor, only a handful have claimed the gift of tongues. That fact does not necessarily invalidate the gift, but it does help keep it in proper perspective. Thousands of believers in those churches have never experienced a miracle beyond the new birth.

To portray miracles as the revival norm is to encourage honest and sincere Christians to try to work up in the flesh what the Holy Spirit has not produced. In some cases, as with the seven sons of Sceva

---

*C. S. Lewis, *Miracles: A Preliminary Study* (New York: Macmillan, 1963).

(Acts 19), the results are ludicrous. In others, they are faith shattering.

A miracle is not authenticated by repetition. Nor is one's spiritual life enhanced by building a tabernacle alongside the memory of a miracle and staying there, trying to recreate the glow. The real test is not what happened then, but what happens afterward. The fruit of the Spirit, according to Galatians 5, is considerably more than a continuing series of charismatic experiences.

(3)When asked if we can duplicate the Indonesian revival in America, the author writes that we can if we will "take out that small computer which is your brain and put it in a little box and shoot it to the moon. Then let God use your heart."*

Even allowing that he is speaking hyperbolically, that still is a dangerous statement. Emotion unrestrained by reason is a risky guide. God has never asked a man to murder his intellect in order to be an instrument of the Holy Spirit.

Instead, Paul counsels us to have renewed minds (Romans 12:1,2). The intellect, renewed and controlled by the Holy Spirit can be a tremendous instrument for good. A person with a "blown mind," whether through drugs, alcohol, or a counterfeit religious experience, throws himself wide open to all kinds of demonic influences.

Deplore with me, if you will, the sterile intellectualism of contemporary Western religion, but you will also agree that renewal is not to be found in dispatching your brain to the moon.

(4)I am concerned that the book portrays an unbalanced relationship between revival and miracles

---

*Mel Tari, *Like a Mighty Wind* (Wheaton: Creation House, 1974).

which could lead well meaning Christians astray. The imbalance is dangerous.

First of all, the astounding humility of the Trinity precludes any exaltation of the Holy Spirit over Christ. Jesus said the "Spirit of truth . . . shall testify of me" (John 15:26). The Godhead is agreed that it is the Son who shall be exalted. The Son magnifies the Father (John 17:4) while the Father honors the Son (Phil 2:9–11) and the Holy Spirit reveals and glorifies Him (John 16:14,15).

Even the gifts of the Spirit are meant to bring about, not the fulness of the Spirit, but the "fulness of Christ" (Eph 4:11–13) in the believer. Paul's admonition to "be filled with the Spirit" is an imperative plea for the appropriation of the Spirit's presence, not a reference to his gifts.

In some mysterious way, any exaltation of the gifts and manifestations of the Holy Spirit quenches his power. His purpose is to magnify the Son, and the Spirit is deeply grieved when his own work is itself glorified. How strange is our intoxication with the gifts over the Giver! It is Christ and his redeeming work, not the Holy Spirit and his ministry of gifting the body, which is to be lifted up.

The blessed Holy Spirit will not be exalted over the Son, and *Like a Mighty Army* comes perilously close to doing that.

(5) Finally, our insensitivity to other cultures causes me to be very apprehensive about an invasion of curiosity-seeking Americans in places where miracles accompany revival. For that reason I still decline to report the details of such events when I hear about them. I want to spare my friends the cultural and spiritual shambles we often leave behind in our rush to sample or exploit some new thing. I have already seen enough of this to be appalled at the prospect of more.

In the early days when reports of miracles began to come out of Timor, two Americans heard about one woman who had been greatly used of God. They determined she must come to America. The whole incident was roughly analogous to scouts from Barnum and Bailey looking for a new circus act. These two women traveled to Indonesia, took a boat to Timor, sought out this little Timorese woman, and begged her to accompany them back to the United States.

She could not and did not, but the very fact that she—a simple peasant woman—was sought out by visitors from abroad produced in her such pride that friends say her spiritual recovery has been a slow process. The two Americans returned home oblivious to the damage they had done.

God will be no man's magician and Jesus will not be coaxed into performing tricks for Herod or anyone else.

Today God is giving Asia an unprecedented opportunity to believe. Thrilling movings of the Holy Spirit are reported in several places. Since these areas represent different peoples with diverse cultures and religious backgrounds, we may expect the Holy Spirit to work in a variety of ways to bring about faith.

In evangelism and revival the Holy Spirit is still sovereign. He will choose the place, the people, and the methods. As the wind, the Spirit still "bloweth where it listeth." At times he may appear as a mighty wind. Again his presence may be more like a gentle breeze.

We cannot lock him into a static and stifling mold. But we can depend on one thing. That which is truly his work will always bear the divine markings.

The greatest evidence that a work has been done by God's Spirit is found in redeemed lives, not restructured molecules. The Bible teaches that Satan has power to reorder physical elements and thus produce "miracles." Witch doctors have been doing it for centuries. Only God can change lives redemptively, however. This, then, becomes the acid test of God's presence in a movement.

And for people with a faith mature enough to accept God's miracles without having to seek after a sign, this ought to be enough.

Chapter 5

The King of All Floods

As the end neared for Cambodia in early 1975, the pace of events picked up. Even outside the country I could feel the pressure building. The other nations had decided to write off the little country as not being important to their own national interests. It was obvious the situation was terminal. Only the date remained to be determined.

In my sadness, I felt a strong desire to spend a little more time at the bedside of this one whom I loved unashamedly. I wanted to see my Khmer brothers and sisters, to feel their heartbeat, to let them know that someone cared very much what was happening. And I wanted to encourage our World Vision staff of nearly 200 people—about 10 of whom were expatriates from Australia, New Zealand, Great Britain, and the U.S.A.

It was for those reasons I decided to swing by Phnom Penh on my way home from India.

So on Saturday, March 1, I found myself on an embassy supply flight from Bangkok to Phnom Penh. Within minutes after I had stepped off the old C-46 at Pochentong Airport, dust and debris leaped skyward about 200 yards away. Another Khmer Rouge rocket had found its target. Since the rockets often

My last conversation with Minh Tien Voan, our associate director in Cambodia, was behind sandbags during a rocket attack on Phnom Penh's Pochentong airport. When I evacuated his family, he chose to stay and serve. No word has been heard from him.

67

came in pairs, about ten of us dived for a bunker. Sixty seconds later another rocket slammed into the Cambodian earth nearby.

You don't have to be a military genius to know when to get a move on, so we headed out quickly even though we couldn't be sure any other place in the city would be more secure. But the airport was always a prime target, with the Khmer Rouge less than two miles away.

The situation had deteriorated seriously since my last visit. The dry season offensive by the communists was on again, as regular as nature itself. The bruised capital was completely isolated by land. The life-giving Mekong River had been cut in three places. No roads were open. Rice and fuel were coming in only by air. Before 1970 and the beginning of the war, the population of Phnom Penh had been about 700,000. Now it exceeded two million—most of the increase was refugees and virtually the entire population was hurting and hungry.

As soon as the church leaders heard I was in town, they came by the hotel. It was a happy reunion, but they were surprised to see me. Almost all the movement these days was outgoing. Would I preach at Bethany Church the next morning?

I would indeed. But what would I say to a group of believers who are gathered together for what might be their last service of praise and worship? What kind of encouragement could I give them?

Sunday morning was, as usual, hot and sticky. We felt it inside the church since there was no electricity to turn the fans. Power was generated only a few hours each evening—if then—because of the critical fuel shortage. As I sat on the platform in the little sanctuary, I was deep in thought and prayer. One by one they came in—Khmer brothers and sisters whom

I had come to love deeply during our five-year relationship.

The church filled quickly. Soon it was jam-packed. Most of the people were relatively new converts. My mind raced back over five years when there was only a handful of Christians in the country. In the past two years the church had exploded with new members. I thanked God it had been my privilege to witness this demonstration of his sovereign power.

The pastor led in prayer. The congregation sang hymns of praise to their Lord and Savior. One was my favorite, *All the Way My Savior Leads Me.* I prayed hard and asked God to give me the right words. His words. In less than twenty-four hours I would be gone. I had a passport to get out. For my brothers and sisters, there was no escape. They would remain under a new regime that would not only seek to blot out the name of Jesus Christ, but would even try to obliterate from the land the centuries-old traditions of Buddhism. To the communists, all religions are an opiate of the people.

But my friends would have to stay. When the rice was gone, they would go hungry. When their homes were attacked, they would bury their dead. Some of them—only God knew how many—would die.

This was going to be an extraordinary service for us all. I prayed for strength to control my emotions so that my deep personal feelings would not get in the way of what the Holy Spirit wanted to say. As one would do with the terminally ill, we did not speak directly of the inevitable. The text to which the Lord led me was Psalm 29:10: *"The Lord sitteth upon the flood; yea, the Lord sitteth King forever."*

I reminded my Khmer brothers and sisters that the whole history of the church has been a history of floods—turmoil, upheavals, persecutions, and martyrdom. There were those times when the church seemed to disappear completely. But during those times of darkness, God never abdicated his sovereign Kingship.

As I looked out on the beautiful faces of these friends whom I might never see again on earth, my emotions nearly spilled over. Many of them had already suffered much for their faith. All were aware that it could happen again. I tried to encourage them to remember that even though our earthly relationship might come to an end, it would not mean that God had left his throne—*"the Lord sitteth King forever."*

I shared the story of Noah and his flood as it is told in the Book of Genesis. God had created such an incredibly beautiful, good world and had put in it a man and woman—his crowning creative act. Yet after a few short generations, the whole creation was in rebellion. The tragedy is described in Genesis 6:11: "The earth also was corrupt before God, and the earth was filled with violence." God purposed to destroy the earth, the creation he had fashioned with such care. But tucked away in verse 8 of that chapter is a glorious note of affirmation: "But Noah found grace in the eyes of the Lord."

Grace is God's undeserved favor. The message: Wrath and judgment would be tempered with mercy. No matter how deep or how consuming the flood, God is still the King who bestows unmerited favor on his people.

It was my prayer, I told them, that the believers in Cambodia would find grace in the eyes of the Lord. The flood might be very deep and very long. It might seem to sweep away all evidence of the knowledge of God, but hidden away in some "ark" would be those on whom the Lord had shined with his grace.

I shared the story of two more "floods." Revelation

18 tells of the destruction of Babylon, the apocalyptic name given to the whole worldly system. It is an event yet to come at the end time when the political and economic systems will collapse from the weight of their own corruption. The whole earth will be in a state of upheaval. The Bible indicates it will be a terrible time.

Revelation 18 is a bleak and terrifying chapter for those whose trust is in this world. But the encouragement and victory come in the next chapter for it shows the destruction of Babylon to have been the work of God's hand, avenging the blood of his servants which had been shed by those wicked worldly systems. The song of triumph which emerges out of the holocaust confirms God's Kingship: *"Alleluia: for the Lord God omnipotent reigneth"* (Revelation 19:6).

The third flood was the flood of Calvary. From the human standpoint, the death of Jesus was a total tragedy. All the hate of hell ascended from the pit and hurled itself against the cross that awesome afternoon at Jerusalem. When the raging torrent ceased, the Son of God was dead. His body was placed in a grave and for three days earth and heaven said nothing.

The silence was terrifying for the disciples. They thought God had abdicated. But on the third day God spoke—eloquently, dramatically, authoritatively through the resurrection and the empty tomb! God was still King.

I reminded my friends there may be a period of time when the voice of God will be heard no longer in the land. I weep to think that now is such a time. But I told them that no matter how long the silence may be, no matter how dark the circumstances may be, God will still be sitting King of that flood.

I gave the congregation an opportunity to respond. Twenty or so raised their hands, saying they wanted to become followers of Jesus for the long ordeal that lay ahead. I had tried to give them a message of hope in an hour of great despair. For the believer the message is always one of hope, regardless of the uncertainties of life or the wickedness of men.

Later than Sunday, I led a communion service for our foreign staff on the World Vision medical, agricultural, and administrative teams. What a magnificent group they were! They had worked under pressures that should have been unbearable, but they had borne them. To my mind they were the most skilled, dedicated, courageous team in the world. How I loved them.

Ten of us sat around a small table in the living room of the nurses' quarters. We stayed away from the windows because the house next door had been hit by a rocket a few days before. We sat quietly— yes, peacefully—in the midst of war. One by one each reflected on the ministry God had made possible in Cambodia.

Dr. Penelope Key, a skilled British doctor, had headed our medical team for eighteen months. She had worked under incredible difficulties. But she didn't talk about those this morning.

In substance, here is what she said:

"Yesterday in my clinic at the refugee center, there were more than five hundred mothers with their sick children, waiting for their turn. Some will come again tomorrow, and some the next day. I chose two to three hundred children from among them. The rest are unchosen.

"There is agony for me in this choosing. When I put up my hand at the end of a five-hour morning stretch, when I call to my doctors, nurses, and clerks, 'That child is the last one for the morning,' what am I doing or saying to the child after the last one? The anguish of the mother whose child is refused haunts me and my staff. Her face stays with us as we eat our lunch, knowing that she is waiting and watching her child.

"Sometimes a waiting child dies while I am away resting. How then can I rest—or eat, or sleep? How can I not choose to see that child? Why did I choose to stop at the child before that one? If I had chosen to see one more child, that child might be alive today.

"All these children are God's little ones. He loves and cares about every one of them. I believe he wants every one of them cared for. He does not want me to choose one from another. He loves them all. But I can care for only one at a time. How do I choose which one?"

I tried to say something, but it really wasn't an answer. I didn't know, and still don't know, if there is an answer.

Carl Harris, World Vision's director in Cambodia, began to speak quietly. He told about his little Khmer namesake, Carl, who had died just a few weeks previously:

"I met Carl on my birthday last August. He was presented to me at our medical team villa while I was opening packages. He was in a covered wicker basket of such small dimensions that it looked like a birthday gift.

"He was the smallest child I had ever seen. His head seemed the size of a tennis ball. The rest of his body was minuscule and he weighed only one kilogram, about 2.2 pounds. He had been abandoned recently at our Tuol Kauk nutrition center when he was probably only thirty-five to forty hours old. Because he had no name known to us, he was, perhaps whimsically, called Carl by the nurses.

"As you know, my job keeps me behind a desk more hours than I'd care to admit. At times, I get stale and feel out of touch with the people we are helping. Therefore, as part of my 'reality therapy' I have often visited the nutrition center. On those visits I sometimes saw Carl and sometimes did not. It depended on his schedule and mine.

"The staff told me he seemed to be fighting the good fight. Physically, he was up and down—sometimes on his way to health and sometimes dangerously near death.

"Unknown to me during those months, and only revealed to me much later, was the fact that to the staff of the center, and to others among our World Vision team, he had become a very special child. He was special as himself, but also special because he represented all the children our medical staff tries to keep alive.

"The last time I saw Carl was Christmas Eve. I had been working on a sermon that afternoon and had begun to feel the staleness of being out of touch.

"I went to the center at 6:30 P.M. to re-feel what was going on. I visited many of the children with Dr. Key, and as a sort of afterthought also visited Carl. He looked in poor physical shape, but was apparently better off than some weeks ago. At any rate, he was bellowing with some gusto and that seemed to be a good sign.

"Two hours later while I was at a Christmas reception, Carl died. The day after Christmas, I conducted his funeral.

"At the burial grounds about twenty kilometers from Phnom Penh, I began the service with the powerful words from the Episcopal Book of Common Prayer: 'I am the resurrection and the life.' And in anticipation of things to come, I read, 'They shall hunger no more, neither thirst any more.' This phrase threatened to unman me as I remembered the previous context of Carl's life.

"Finally, I ended the most meaningful funeral I have ever attended with the prayer:

'O God, whose most dear Son did take little children into his arms and bless them; give us grace, we beseech thee, to entrust the soul of this child to thy never-failing care and love, and bring us all to thy heavenly kingdom; through the name of thy Son, Jesus Christ our Lord. Amen.' "

Others spoke from their hearts. Few eyes were dry as we ministered to each other.

Then we shared the bread and the wine. The words still ring in my memory . . . This is my body . . . This is my blood . . . Take, eat; take, drink.

We sang a hymn and said good-bye.

As I left, one of the nurses from Australia, Sandra Menz, slipped a letter into my pocket. I didn't have time to open it until I was on the plane to Bangkok.

Here is what it said:

Nothing so disturbs our rest and takes away our peace of mind as physical and spiritual fear. . . . Our Lord, who wished the best for us, that we might be full of joy and peace, would have us altogether free from fear. Not only have we this loving command, 'Fear not,' but we are graciously given a threefold reason for obeying this Divine injunction: " . . . I have redeemed thee, I have called thee by My name: thou art Mine" (Isaiah 43:1). We are His redeemed ones, His own purchased possession, known individually to the One who died for us. With His wonderful words ringing in our ears we can fearlessly face the future, knowing that it is in His hands.

And I thought I had gone to Phnom Penh to encourage *them!* There are no floods deep enough to quench that kind of spirit.

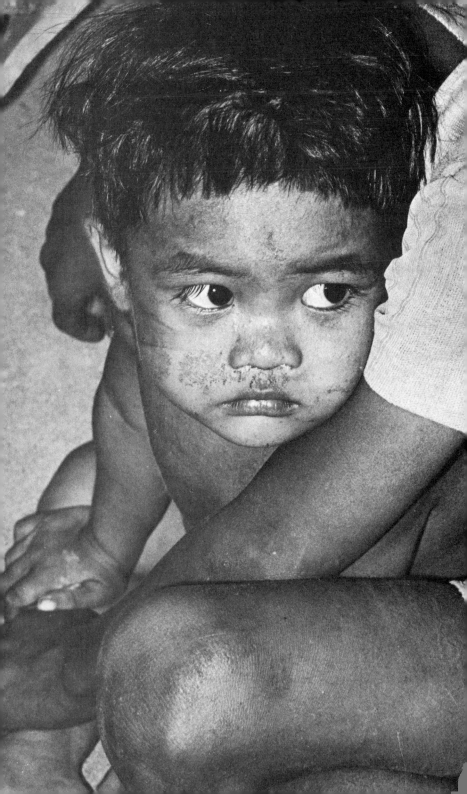

Chapter 6

Where Only Man Is Vile

 cinched up my seat belt and held on for dear life as the pilot put our helicopter into a series of very tight circles to gain enough altitude to be beyond the reach of rebel guns below. Over the right gunner's shoulder through the open door, I could see the school yard where we had landed a few hours earlier dropping away as we climbed higher.

At the safe altitude of 1,000 feet the pilot came out of his corkscrew maneuver and headed south. This procedure had been adopted after the military had lost several planes and helicopters to rebel rifle fire at low altitudes during normal landings.

As we climbed higher and the village grew smaller, I thought about those we had left behind there. There were nearly 4,000 homeless families, sick and malnourished children, weary social workers, and one lone evangelical pastor. They were protected by a handful of soldiers who had managed to secure an area about three miles square around the village.

It wasn't Vietnam or Cambodia.

This was the Philippines.

In 1973, the *Far Eastern Economic Review* was calling the civil war in Mindanao "Marcos' Vietnam." With my World Vision colleagues Mel Van Peursem,

This child of a Muslim refugee on the island of Mindanao sits on the floor with his father. In conflicts like the civil war in Mindanao, it is always the children who suffer the most.

77

Bob Larson, and Bill Kliewer, I was there in response to an urgent call for help. It had come on behalf of tens of thousands of refugees who were innocent victims of a vicious political/cultural/religious conflict which threatened to completely engulf this Filipino island.

As we flew over the incredibly beautiful islands in the Moro Gulf and along the Mindanao coast, I couldn't get out of my mind the ugly scenes we had just witnessed. I remembered the little girl pushing rice into her mouth past the dead flies which lay in spittle around her teeth. I saw again the mothers in one refugee center (read "warehouse") sitting around on boxes trying to nurse their babies from dry withered breasts. I recalled the villagers, driven twice from their homes by attacking gangs called Ilagats (Rats) who burned and pillaged until nothing was left.

And the words of the missionary hymn kept coming back to me: " ...where every prospect pleases, and only man is vile." I have seen the sinful and depraved nature of man demonstrated in many ways as I have walked the world, but few situations have been marked with the total violence and vengeance as that manifested in this so-called "religious war."

Externally, the prospect of Mindanao is pleasing. This second largest island in the republic, known as the "Pearl of the Orient Seas," is considered the "land of promise" by the Filipinos. Money crops grow well in its fertile soils and fish abound along the irregular coastline. There are minerals in the mountains of Zamboanga del Norte and oil deposits under the Sulu Sea.

But until recent years it seemed no one cared. The land was largely untapped and untamed. Minority tribes—some, like the recently-discovered Tasadays, still live in the Stone Age—were scattered throughout the remote interior. The coastal areas were inhabited mostly by the Moros (Muslims) who settled there during the fourteenth and fifteenth centuries. For generations they represented the largest ethnic group on Mindanao. They worshiped at the mosques, fished when they felt like it, and grew a little rice over which to pour the fish sauce.

Those who possessed fast boats and a dash of daring took up smuggling as an occupation. There was always a market for the cloth, cigarettes, and carbines which they brought from the East Malaysian state of Sabah on the island of Borneo.

If life could not be described as idyllic, it was—for the most part—at least simple and uncomplicated.

In 1939, life began to change. The sturdy, ambitious, and hardworking Ilacanoes of the north began to migrate south to Mindanao to conquer the rugged land. They prospered and soon the original people saw control of their ancient land threatened.

But the *Cristianoes* (although most of the Ilacanoes are Roman Catholics, this is a loose term which includes most non-Muslims) refused to surrender the land which they had carved out of untamed jungle.

The stand-off spelled trouble.

Muslim gangs called Barracudas and Blackshirts were organized to terrorize Christian villages. The Ilagats were the Christian's answer. Murder, raping, and pillaging have gone on for several years. Each act of violence brought swift revenge.

But the situation took a dangerous shift in 1972. Acting under martial law, President Marcos ordered all unlicensed firearms to be surrendered to the Armed Forces of the Philippines. Many of the Cristianoes brought in their guns, but most of the Muslim men headed for the mountains with their weapons to begin a worrisome and bloody confrontation with the Army. On the island of Basilan, with a population of

200,000, Police Chief Estrada told me not a single Muslim weapon had been surrendered. He quoted a standard Muslim dictum which I had heard before: "I will give up my wife, but not my gun."

Amnesty was offered by President Marcos, but it was ignored. It was extended, but with almost total failure. Thus the stage was set for the civil war which still goes on like a perpetual see-saw. The rebels—no one knows for sure how many there are—are well-armed and trained. It is said they are financed and aided by at least one outside Muslim country. (In 1976, Mrs. Marcos went to Libya in what was reported to be an attempt to reach a settlement.) The Filipino Muslims say they want independence—and, not incidentally, the riches of Mindanao which would come with it.

Marcos knows he cannot afford to lose either the territory or the wealth. Bloody confrontation was inevitable. In the early days, the Muslims were joined by communist rebels (called the "New People's Army") from the northern Philippines whose goal of overthrowing the government could only be enhanced by the trouble in the south.

One of the greatest tragedies resulting from the incendiary situation in Mindanao, as in every other human conflict, is the suffering of the innocent. Uprooted from their lands, driven from their homes, struggling to stay alive, both Christian and Muslim refugees by the scores of thousands (officially called "displaced persons arising from social conflict") trudge to the security of the nearest town. Often the attacks by the rebels are so savage and evacuation by the villagers so hasty, they have to leave their dead unburied.

On the island of Basilan about 80 percent of the Cristiano homes in the mountains were burned down by the Blackshirts. Some who tried to return to get their belongings were killed. The owners of the copra plantations on the island were forced to flee to the towns as many of the plantation workers proved to be in sympathy with the rebels.

We were taken to a school which had been turned into a refugee center. The people had been there three months and only God knew how long they would have to stay. They lived on the floor and only pieces of cloth separated the families. One room so occupied had seen three births in three months, but there had been three deaths also the previous week. In that particular camp, three to five babies die every week.

The local evangelical churches had been assisting both Cristianoes and Muslims. Bill Pamaran, a layman, was head of the relief effort. He told me: "In this hard time the refugees hope for nothing but only food and clothing. If we have that to give, our people are only too willing to volunteer their service for Christ's sake."

Juan Talion, another layman who had given up his business in Cotabato City to serve Christ full-time, told me of a raid by the Blackshirts on the town of Colombo on the main island of Mindanao. It occurred at three o'clock in the afternoon when the schoolteachers were having a general meeting. These women were captured, held hostage in the school, raped as many as fifteen times a day, and made to serve their captors naked. Two of the teachers were able to escape. The terrible ordeal had driven one, a mother of three, out of her mind. When her husband approached her, she began to scream and then committed suicide in her own home.

I cannot forget Juan's sad eyes and halting words as he told us of the shame and terror at Colombo. The vice-mayor of the town is an evangelical Christian who barely escaped with his life. He and his wife fled with their two-year-old son, covering nearly four-teen miles in one day as they crossed the Trojas mountains which reach up to twelve thousand feet in some places.

When asked how they could possibly have done it, his wife answered simply: "There was no other way."

Talion says many evangelical Christians have been killed in Cotabato province. No one has official fig-ures for the slaughter, but it seems certain that more Cristianoes have been killed than Muslims since it is the Muslims who have kept their guns. When the army arrived at Labason, where 37 Christians had been killed, they found 901 empty shells in the village.

Standard procedure for a Muslim raid is to shoot up the village at random, hack and mutilate the bodies with vicious bolo knives, and then behead the victims, children included.

But there are also many innocent Muslim victims as the Ilagats retaliate. So the terrible feud goes on.

During the height of the conflict, I accepted an in-vitation from an interdenominational movement known as "Christ the Only Way" to preach evangel-istic meetings in several towns and cities. None of the places had had any noteworthy previous evangelistic response. We didn't know what to expect during the first of these meetings which was held in Zamboanga City. Situated at the southwestern tip of Mindanao, it is a beautiful town known as "the city of flowers."

Because of its convenient location, it is also famous as the "port of entry" for goods smuggled from Sabah. For such a faraway place, the local market has an amazing selection of merchandise from Europe, Japan, and the United States.

The meetings, sponsored by the local Protestant churches, were held in a downtown park. Open-air evangelism is much more effective among Muslims who are reluctant to go inside even a neutral building to attend a Christian meeting. As darkness descended over our lovely setting each evening, many Muslims would come and stand at the edge of the crowd. Some were among the hundreds who responded to the gospel invitation. At least one young man was thrown out by his parents when he went home and told them he had become a believer in Jesus Christ.

One evening, after I had spoken from the beautiful love story found in the Old Testament book of Hosea, I left the park and got aboard one of the many "jeepneys" which serve as a kind of minibus in the Philippines. When I got off at my hotel and tried to hand the driver a couple of pesos to cover the fare, he refused it. Thinking perhaps he wanted more, I added another peso but still he refused to take it.

Seeing the puzzled look on my face, the driver said in some what broken English: "You are Christian. I am Muslim. I love you." Then he drove away.

Unquestionably, he had heard my message that evening. The incident touched me deeply and when the crusade musical team arrived at the hotel later, I told them the story. Someone remarked that maybe another revolution was taking place in the city—a revolution of love.

The next morning Danniebelle Hall, a talented musician and composer from California and leader of the all-black women's quartet who were providing music for the crusade, announced that she had written a new song. At the meeting that night I told the story of the jeepney driver and asked the group to sing Danniebelle's song. Performed with just a touch of Latin rhythm, it was an immediate hit with the populace.

One of the local radio stations recorded it and used it as a theme song. For months afterwards, the people of Zamboanga—Christian and Muslim alike—were singing:

> There's a revolution of love in Zamboanga,
> You can feel the Spirit moving in the air;
> There's a revolution of love in Zamboanga,
> See the smiling, happy faces everywhere.
> O, I love you, my brother and my sister,
> If you listen you can hear the people say,
> There's a revolution of love in Zamboanga
> And you can join the revolution today.

The song provided the name for a later evangelistic effort which touched some fifteen other cities. Called the "Revolution of Love/Mindanao," it was a joint effort of Christ the Only Way, World Impact, and World Vision. It was a ten-month program designed to demonstrate love in the midst of hate by both word and deed.

The "deed" part of it was handled by multinational teams of Christian young people who went to live in the *barrios* of Mindanao and do social action projects which would demonstrate Christian caring. These students and career young people came from Canada, New Zealand, the United States, and from other parts of the Philippines. Many of them were recruited by Dr. Keith Phillips, president of World Impact, an organization which works primarily in America's inner cities.

For six months these integrated teams worked and witnessed in their areas under the watchcare of the local churches.

Then came the "word" part. Dr. Phillips and I teamed up with several Filipino evangelists for mini-crusades in each of the places. Some of the towns were remote, requiring transportation by bus or boat through unfriendly territory. To make one of his crusades, Keith had to fly on an ancient DC-3 through a typhoon. Getting to one of mine required a three-hour ride across a stretch of ocean infested by both sharks and pirates in what the locals call a "pumboat," a long, narrow canoe powered by a little two-cycle pump motor.

My philosophy about travel is that my safety is God's responsibility. That way I don't immobilize myself by trying to decide if I should or shouldn't. The way I figure it is that hardly any place is more dangerous than a Los Angeles freeway.

Under the leadership of Juan Talion and Doug Cozart, a colleague of mine in World Vision, the preparations for the three-day meetings in each town proceeded in a rather unusual way. As with the earlier meetings in Zamboanga, it was decided to have them outside. It was also decided to give them a completely indigenous character by planning them along the lines of the familiar and popular Filipino political rallies.

Since Paul tells us that our gospel is held in earthen vessels anyway, I have always felt that if that vessel looks familiar to those in each culture, they are more apt to accept it. Too many of the vessels in which the gospel is exported bear the obvious stamp, "Made in the U.S.A."

I've never seen any virtue in that.

So Doug and Juan planned the meetings Filipino-style. The first ingredient in the indigenous recipe was a parade. So on the afternoon of the opening crusade meeting, we would rent all the pedicabs (bicycle taxis) in town and the young people would decorate them with balloons and signs. These were joined by a collection of jeepneys and automobiles, also festooned.

A local band was recruited to lead the parade. What the procession lacked in sophistication, it made up in noise and excitement! As we moved through the town, invitations to the meetings were distributed. By the time the parade wound its way into the outdoor meeting place, we were being followed by one to two thousand people.

The second ingredient for a local flavor was a talent show. The first hour was given to a display of local talent. Some had been previously arranged by the organizing team, but other numbers were performed spontaneously. In one town a man sang a Muslim love song and in another we had a young hula dancer! As the performers received the appreciative applause of their friends and fellow townspeople, the noise attracted even more people.

Every meeting became a gala event!

When the talent show came to an end, a musical group from the Far East Broadcasting Company in Manila would take the stage and sing gospel songs. Now the crowd began to quiet down and soon it was time for the sermon and the invitation to receive Jesus Christ. The people were always respectful, never disorderly.

Scores and hundreds of people responded in every meeting. Among them were numbers of Muslims. In some towns we received official Roman Catholic support. Their schools were open to members of our team and in one town I was asked by the local monsignor, who sat on the platform during our first crusade meeting, if I would speak at his early Mass on Sunday morning. I accepted enthusiastically. I was still happy but less enthusiastic when I found out it was at 6:30. The evangelical service didn't start until ten!

After the first Mass, attended by about a thousand people, the monsignor asked if I would also speak at the next service. There were about 1,200 for that one.

At ten o'clock I went to the evangelical church and preached to 46.

The work of the youth teams in preparation and follow-up proved to be very effective, building on the relationships they had established. The social action projects on which they worked were tangible demonstrations of caring love. One of the projects of the team in Lamitan, on Basilan Island, was making and placing trash cans on the streets throughout the town to encourage civic cleanliness. Each container—beautifully painted—carried the ROL/M emblem.

The loving concern shown by the churches in Mindanao opened wide the door for the Christian witness to Muslims. There is no way to assess the long-range impact of what took place during that time, but certainly the immediate impact was noticeable.

The Rev. José Nabob, pastor of the Zamboanga Evangelical Church, summed it up beautifully with these words:

"We are being welcomed now. Our love has destroyed their hate!"

So it has always been.

Even where man is vile, *that* prospect pleases.

Chapter 7   A Green Thumb Grows in Kenya

Two American tourists—florists from Seattle, Washington—arrived in Nairobi, Kenya, in 1968.

They bought their jungle attire in a local shop, loaded up with film, and set off for an animal safari that would make them the envy of all the folks back home.

Denny and Jeanne Grindall saw and enjoyed East Africa's abundant fauna, but this couple from University Presbyterian Church also saw something which changed the course of their lives and is in the process of changing the life style of a people.

They saw the Masai, the brown-skinned herders of the East African plains.

Seven years had passed when I met Denny for the first time in the coffee shop of a Nairobi hotel. We were introduced by our mutual Masai friend, the Rev. John Mpaayei, then of the Kenya Bible Society. A few hours later, propelled along by Denny's boundless energy, we were in a Land Rover and I was headed for an unscheduled visit to meet his adopted people.

So many exciting things that have happened in my life seem to have been "unscheduled"—by me, at least.

Masai tribeswomen stand in front of a ferro-cement "house" designed by Denny Grindall to replace their traditional mud-and-dung huts. They are a primitive people trying to keep their equilibrium while moving into the twentieth century.

COME WALK THE WORLD

It was an easy trip out of Nairobi at first. They all are—at first. Good paved roads. Then, as always happens eventually, we took "the road to the right." Leaving the blacktop behind us, we moved out over the dirt, dust, and potholes into the African bush. All I could see for miles around was scrub grass and jagged rocks.

This was Masai-land.

For a cultural anthropologist the Masai fall into the neat scientific category of "Nilo-Hamite." To the late nineteenth-century Scottish explorer, Joseph Thomson, they were diseased, illiterate, uncivilized. To *National Geographic*, they are splendor in Kodachrome.

To Denny and Jeanne they are their new family.

It all started when some Presbyterian missionaries invited the Grindalls to see some of the efforts among the Masai before the tourist couple left Nairobi after their animal safari. Denny and Jeanne were appalled at what they saw in the villages. "Houses" made of mud and cow dung. Sick children living with flies and filth. (Half the babies died before the age of four.) Malnourished mothers trying to nurse malnourished babies. Carcasses of dead animals littering the landscape.

No vision was necessary to see what the Masai needed. Or maybe what their eyes saw *was* the vision. Desperate need for hygiene. Nutrition. Water. Hope.

The Grindalls were moved, but they had their own plans. Those plans focused on a quiet retreat in the Pacific Northwest as a present to themselves for a life of hard work.

But their exposure to the Masai was like steel to magnet. In 1969, Denny and Jeanne were back in Kenya. Each year since then they have spent six months in Kenya and six months in Seattle growing and selling flowers—and raising money so they can help the Masai the other six months.

As we bounced along in the Land Rover, Denny pointed far into the distance. "See that patch of water? That's the dam. That's where we're going." Within an hour we had arrived, but it was later I realized I had been on a trip that changed a bit of my life, too.

I don't know if it was Denny or the Masai. Undoubtedly both.

The Masai are cattle people. They have no written history, so everything we know about them has come from oral traditions. For more than a thousand years this proud tribal group has roamed the wild East African plains of Kenya and Tanzania.

Their whole existence revolves around their herds. A normal greeting for a Masai is, "I hope your cattle are well." In the early hours of each new day, Masai women pray to Venus, the morning star. They chant: "I pray you who rises yonder to hear me. Keep our cows alive." The men remind each other: "God gave us cattle and grass. Cattle are in our hearts. Their smell is in our nostrils."

They pray to the god Ngai. The prayers are sincere, but in recent days those prayers have fallen on stone ears. Drought, disease, and overgrazing have wiped out whole herds. Venus has not looked with favor on the Masai people.

If Masai life revolves around cattle, inevitably it revolves even more critically around water. Both the tribespeople and Denny knew this. For centuries this search for water for their cattle has made nomadic wanderers out of the Masai.

With Denny's coming, the pattern is changing. He has helped them build earth-filled dams, designed a simple and easy-to-clean permanent house, introduced vegetables along with the milk-and-blood diet, encouraged them to have fewer but healthier cattle, and taught them to keep the cattle in *kraals* outside the village living compound to control flies and disease.

But it hasn't all been easy. At first this blond man from the West—whom the Masai call "Simba" (Swahili for lion) because of the hair on his arms—was viewed with some suspicion. Traditionally, the Masai have been among the most anticolonial of Kenya's tribes. But slowly, as they sensed the genuineness of the Grindalls, acceptance of the outsiders increased. Today when Denny and Jeanne are in Kenya, they live in a Masai village in one of the little ferro-cement "igloos" Denny has designed to replace the mud-and-dung houses.

From suspicion . . . to acceptance . . . to adoption.

For starters, Denny and Jeanne determined they would not hand out doles to the Masai. They insisted the people be largely responsible for their own projects.

After the first dam was built and a permanent village established on the banks of the little lake which it formed, a group of Masai herders came to Denny and said, "We have seen what the people here have done and we would also like water for our cattle. Will you come and help us build a dam?"

Denny responded by telling them if they were willing to sell some of their cattle for the project, he would take a look at the possibilities when they had brought him the money from the first cattle sale. That was asking them to break a tradition of centuries, for a Masai sells his cows only in direst emergency. But Denny knew they had to be serious about the project and invest as much as they could themselves.

Two weeks later the same group of men returned and produced 17,000 Kenyan shillings, almost $2,300.

They placed the money in his hands, saying, "Here is the first payment."

"Then every week, four men would come to our house with a little tin box filled with hundred-shilling notes folded eight ways," Denny told me. "It seemed like it took us hours just to get the money unfolded! When they had brought enough money I went over to their valley. We built the dam together. Now they have clean water. They no longer need to roam all over the plains in search of water for their thirsty animals. In this case, as in most, the Masai paid 80 to 90 percent of the cost of the project."

That initial gesture especially pleased Denny because he could remember when he was building the first earth-filled dam. He and a group of Masai men were scooping up the earth and piling it in great mounds. Another group of men watched scornfully.

"You are pouring your kettle into the earth," they laughed, which is a Masai saying that—loosely translated—means "You've wasted all your wealth."

But when the rains came and the dam filled—and stayed filled—the skeptics became believers overnight. "Now," says Denny, "they say absolutely nothing is impossible."

Simeon, a 61-year-old Masai patriarch, summed it up simply: "If you explain things to us, then we can understand."

The old chief stood regally and ramrod straight, colorful beads hanging from one ear, as we talked about life on the arid Kenya plains. Simeon knows quite a bit about drought. He recalls one of the worst years: "We had no water for our cattle here, so we had to drive them about twelve miles across the plains until we found a stream. Then we turned around and came home. We did this every other day for several months. But each time more animals died. No cow could survive in that kind of drought. I lost

500 head of cattle. My friend, Jonah, had 750 cows. At the end of the drought, he could count only seven."

Now Simeon's village—and a growing number of others—has a lake, gravity-fed pipelines, irrigation, and clean drinking water.

"Their lives changed completely in just one year," says Denny without exaggeration. "They *want* to have a better life. Chief Simeon said to me, 'Even if I'm old, I would rather work—even if I die working—so that our children and our children's children will remember what has been done here.'"

But others have come to the Masai before and little, if anything changed. Why, I asked Denny, is it different this time?

"Because everything we do must be self-help," he responded. "We insist they do the work themselves. We feel it is a mistake to go out and just do things for people, spend money, and say, we're going to do this and that *for* you.

"The Masai people respond to this. Missionaries have come in and preached to somebody on a Sunday and left and come back two weeks later and preached again. The people have really stayed right where they were. They've never had a chance to know anything better.

"They have said to me, 'Denny, why do you and Jeanne come out here? We know you get no pay, that you're doing it entirely on your own. Why?'

"This gives us a chance to tell them what Christ means in our lives. And what he can do in theirs."

That's been the Grindalls' aim from the outset. Alongside the community development projects, eight churches have been built. Some congregations still worship under trees as they wait to get enough money to build a small structure. Masai evangelists move from village to village sharing the good news of the gospel. Over 100 tribespeople have been baptized —unprecedented in the years of mission work among them—and many more have come to know Jesus as Lord.

Chief Simeon is one of those believers. He believes now both in Jesus and in the possibility of a new, less precarious way of living for his Masai people. The latter step of faith was almost more difficult than the first.

Denny tells the story:

"It rains here only two months each year—April and May. We had removed the earth for the dam, packed it around the sides and waited for the rains. This was the supreme test. Would the dam hold? Simeon had his doubts.

"The rains started to pound the dam. Slowly the reservoir behind began to fill. It rained and stormed all night.

"In the middle of the night, Simeon did something no Masai ever does. He left his hut in the pitch black of night and slowly edged his way to the dam. This is unheard of because the Masai know there are lions everywhere. No Masai is ever outside alone at night.

"Simeon was positive the dam would wash away. When he approached the edge of the dam he couldn't believe his eyes. The dam was still there and the lake was filling fast. Two weeks later, most of the people were still in a state of shock to see all that water. For three weeks the water flowed continually through a 24-inch pipe.

"This dam cost $10,000. The villagers paid $8,000 of the total cost."

Denny is obviously proud and pleased. And he should be. This is self-help at its best.

Jeanne is teaching the women to bake bread, to sew and to care for their children in more hygienic ways. She has 165 women in one class alone.

Denny continues to put his green thumb into previously parched Masai land. The result is zucchini,
carrots, parsnips, spinach, chard, beets, onions, and
cucumbers. You name it, and Denny is trying to grow
it—successfully, most of the time.

This, too, is part of Denny's experiment. Traditionally, the Masai have never eaten vegetables.
Their diet came exclusively from their cattle. As we
walked throught the lush, orderly community garden
where Simeon's wife was watering from a five-gallon
can, the old cattleman told me, "Because of Denny,
we know good things can come from the ground, too."

The list of completed and proposed projects among
the Masai is almost endless. The price tag for each is
thought of in terms of cattle rather than money. If a
Masai sells five cows, he will have enough money to
build a permanent house of ferro-cement.

Churches and schools are joint ventures for the
whole village. For centuries Masai women have carried water for miles on their backs. Often the water-
holes have been more than five miles from their
homes. Now thousands of feet of pipeline bring water
to a tap outside a Masai house.

Jonah, one of Denny's best friends, said with a
smile on his face, "Now we know the women will be
at home!" Since he has three wives, that is not an in-
consequential result of having running water. Jonah
says now that he's a Christian he won't take any more
wives.

"Besides," he adds, still smiling, "I can't afford it."

Much of what has been done with the Masai can
easily be called a "success story." People's lives have
been radically changed. The villages where Denny
and Jeanne work have better sanitation. There is less
malaria than before. Less dysentery. Less eye disease.
Fewer small babies crawl into smoldering fires be-

cause safer stoves have been built. Masai churches are beginning to dot the countryside.

But all this is still only a beginning. There are tens of thousands of Masai who continue to live in filth and disease. Their cattle die during the periodic droughts. Women continue to spend their strength walking many miles to a stream for a small jug of precious water.

And most of the Masai are still waiting to hear of him who said, "Whoever drinks of the water that I shall give him, shall never thirst."

Speaking of the two American tourists who came to see the wildlife and stayed to adopt a people and a land, Chief Simeon says: "God must have spoken to Denny. It must have been God who told him to come from his own country to help the people of this place."

"If you have someone else like Denny and Jeanne in your country, please send them to us."

Chapter 8 The Angry Winds of Andhra

Mr. Sundara Rao sent his students home early that Saturday. A drizzle had already set in and the gusting winds twisted the palm fronds, confirming the radio report that the cyclone had shifted away from Madras and was headed northeast toward the coast of Andhra Pradesh.

He could not have known then what terror that night held for him and millions of other people who live in the fertile "rice bowl" of eastern India.

During that time of year the Indian Ocean frequently spawns cyclonic winds which spin into the Bay of Bengal, sometimes hitting India and at other times roaring into the low delta of Bangladesh. The people have learned to live with them the same way residents of Florida's east coast live with their annual hurricanes. Sometimes the cyclones are merely nuisances but occasionally they turn into real killers.

Not since 1864 had the combination of a cyclone and tidal wave hit India.

Not until November 19, 1977.

G. Kalyama Sundara Rao, a postgraduate teacher, intended to leave the school right after the students, but some last minute chores delayed him so that it was one o'clock before he was free. Although the

Sitting in the rubble of the church where Ravi and Kotammi's parents died when the cyclone struck, I promised we would become their family and provide for them.

storm had increased in intensity when he started off on his bicycle, he was sure he could make it to his village of Murty Rakshana Nagar, only three miles away.

But pedaling against the wind proved impossible. In fact, he lost ground as the gusts blew him backwards. Leaving his bicycle in a shop, he caught a bus, but soon chose to abandon it as well when a large tree blown across the road blocked their progress.

Over the warnings of the conductor and driver he left the bus and plunged out into the whirling maelstrom, determined to reach the home of a friend only fifty yards away where he could wait out the storm.

It took him more than half an hour to negotiate that distance, but he never made it to his friend's house. Before leaving the bus, the teacher had taken off his shoes. A strong gust tore them and an umbrella out of his grasp.

"I wanted to try to save them," he told me, "but the wind turned me in another direction. I couldn't go where I wanted to go; I was at the mercy of the wind. Somehow I stumbled across my shoes and umbrella, but by this time I could not find my way. The air was filled with water. I couldn't see and I had trouble breathing. Each breath and each step could be taken only with the greatest effort.

"I thought I would suffocate. It was getting dark and the wind was blowing harder. People ran from a collapsing house and I followed them into the house next door. We huddled in one small room with only a piece of candle for light until someone made a kerosene lamp from a bottle and a piece of cloth.

"About six in the evening, water began to rise in the room. This was the first time I had thought about the possibility of a tidal wave. Immediately my mind went to my family down the road and I was sure they were dead. Mentally I tried to prepare myself to go the next morning and count the bodies of my wife, my children, and my mother.

"I said, 'God, everything is over!'

"That must have been about the middle of the cyclone. The people in the room wanted someone to pray. All I could say was, 'God, you have shown us your might; now show us your mercy.'

"I think I slept a little, but it seemed more like a trance perhaps brought on by emotional exhaustion. I remember that about 12:30 midnight everything suddenly became quiet and still. The wind had died down. I looked outside and saw that the sky was clear.

"Even the stars were shining, but the scene they illuminated was one of death and destruction. I ran toward my house, but it took me four hours of struggle through mud, water, debris, and fallen trees to get there.

"You cannot imagine my joy when I heard my second daughter call out, 'Look! Dad's coming!' My family was all safe! Our house was badly damaged, but we were alive. There was a lot of crying, but the tears were tears of joy. God had truly been merciful."

Not all the tears shed that morning were caused by joyful reunions. When the sun came up over the Indian Ocean coastline it revealed a scene not unlike that which remains after an atomic blast. An Indian scientist investigating the storm said, "The energy unleashed by the tropical cyclone with high velocity is equal to the energy released by the explosion of 200 hydrogen bombs."

When I went in a few days later with our DART team (Disaster Assistance and Reporting Team), I had to admit I have never seen anything like it. I am not a stranger to the destruction of war or natural disasters, but I have never seen anything else that better qualified for the phrase "total devastation."

Estimates of the extent of destruction—including the loss of human life—can be only guessed at. Perhaps 250,000 work animals perished. Over 2,000 villages and hamlets were destroyed. Two million people were left homeless.

Although the area is considered to be the third most densely populated in all of India, the death count was reported deceptively low—under 20,000—because of the political rivalries between the state and central governments. Bishop Andhra Rao Samuel, moderator of the Church of South India whose diocese is in the cyclone area, told me he thought 100,000 would be a more accurate figure.

Samachar, the Indian press agency, reported 20,000 dead on the island of Divi alone.

One reason for the high total was the presence of thousands of migrant workers from other parts of Andhra Pradesh who were in the coastal area for the annual rice harvest which was just beginning. Four thousand were in Divi. Most were washed out to sea by the receding tidal wave.

The storm did its worst damage in an area about 350 miles wide and 50 miles deep. The tidal wave itself swept inland up to 16 miles, with water reaching a height of from 20 to 30 feet. Seagoing fishing vessels were left stranded on dry land ten miles from the ocean. Tens of thousands of acres of rich farmland were made nonproductive for up to five years by the salt water.

At least 80 percent of the rice harvest was lost although workers were trying to salvage some of it from the mud.

But to really understand the effects of a disaster, you must see it in terms of people. And that's what I was in India to do. It was a difficult assignment. The enormity of the destruction kept overshadowing the personal tragedies. And the logistical problems of trying to bring relief to tens of thousands in isolated hamlets made it nearly impossible to concentrate on individual needs.

More than a few times, however, my heart would be deeply moved by the plight of a single person and I would find myself emotionally and personally involved. But always there was the frustrating awareness of being just one person with limited means. The only consolation during those times was in remembering that God never expects us to do more than our human limitations make possible.

But I found I couldn't be satisfied with doing any less than that, either.

One morning as we drove through the devastated land, I saw a sight that gripped me. I don't know why this one man should have caught my attention any more than the thousands of others we had passed. He was sitting on a makeshift cot . . . maybe fifty feet off the road . . . all alone . . . the pieces of his small hut lying broken and scattered around him.

His white beard sharply contrasted with his brown wrinkled face, but it matched the thin piece of cotton around his midsection, which was all he had to cover his dark nakedness. I didn't want to delay our relief caravan, which was on its way to the large village of Mandapalka, so I said nothing. But about a hundred yards down the road, I told the driver to stop. I suddenly remembered that a priest and Levite had once passed by such a man in their hurry to do "religious" work.

I walked back down the road to where he sat. Perhaps, "road" is too grand a name for it. Actually, it was nothing more than a set of tracks atop a five-foot levee. The tidal wave had piled debris, animal carcasses, and human bodies on the levee to heights up to ten feet. Soldiers cleared the tracks by moving the tangled mass to either side and setting the whole thing to the torch. Smoke still rose from the funeral pyres and I pressed a moth ball to my nose to counteract the overpowering odor of decaying flesh and burning bodies.

I approached the old man gently, for it seemed almost obscene to me that his grief and agony ... his pitifully few possessions ... his nothingness ... should lie exposed for all the world to see. He looked so fragile ... so helplessly alone ... so inconsolably sad.

I knelt before Enkataswami (for he told me that was his name), laid my hand on his bony fingers, and said quietly, "Tell me about it." Tears filled the eyes and wet the cheeks of this 75-year-old grandfather as he told me of the terrifying night when the angry winds ripped children from their father's strong arms ... of the wall of water with fire on top which swept everything away ... of the deathly silence throughout the land when the night of terror had ended.

"What do you mean by 'a wall of water with fire on top'?" I asked him. He simply repeated it again. He knew about tidal waves, but he had never seen this phenomenon before. His mention of the fire explained the scorched trees I had seen, their leaves burned brown.

A 50-year-old woman and her nephew were clinging to the top of a palmyra tree, their bodies in the swirling salt water, when they saw a "huge red ball of fire." Some people were reported to have had their faces blackened by the fire.

Such a "sea fire" had never before been reported in India, but it is said to have occurred in connection with the Florida Keys hurricane in 1935. A standard text, *Atlantic Hurricanes* by Gordon Dunn and Banner Miller, says the fire is an electrical display caused by "a myriad of minute electrostatic discharges which appear like millions of tiny fireflies." These apparently originate as a result of frictionally generated static electricity, as literally millions of tiny sand particles are picked up and driven along by the hurricane winds.

Enkataswami could not have known of the scientific origin of the strange fire nor was it likely to be of more than casual interest to him. My aged friend was too consumed by his personal loss . . . all eight of his grandchildren . . . plus both daughters-in-law . . . and the homes and meager belongings of his sons with whom he lived.

"I should have died as well," he told me, "for now I have nothing to live for."

There was no way I could replace his family, but neither could I leave him without doing something. I found out that it would cost about 100 rupees to replace the palmyra thatch on his roof, so I slipped him that amount which he tucked into his loincloth. It represented only about $12 for me, but for him it was the equivalent of two months' wages for one of his sons.

It seemed that everyone had a story to tell. Some of them had happy endings. More often, the storyteller finished in tears of grief. In the same village where the schoolteacher lived, I met a young mother who was holding a small baby. Friends told me the infant had survived by a miracle. The night of the storm, when the baby was only six days old, the mother ran with her baby to seek protection in stronger buildings. As she fell trying to cross the railroad tracks, the baby was snatched from her arms by the wind. Certain that her baby had perished, and injured herself by the fall, she allowed friends to take her to a hospital where she spent the night.

The next morning a search party went out to bring back the body of her baby. Instead they found the child very much alive and they restored him to his joyous mother. She has decided to change his name to Moses because, like the Old Testament miracle baby, her child too was "drawn from the water."

But in the same village I had prayer with a young mother and father whose infant was blown from their arms as they fled their collapsing house. That baby died.

The rampaging storm seemed to select its victims in a random, capricious manner. Some who went into churches were killed, while in the village of Mandapalka (the name means "shelter for a flock") more than a hundred people survived the tidal wave by climbing to the top of a Hindu temple. Just a couple of hundred yards away some eighty people were trapped inside a block building by the rising water and drowned.

At the edge of Mandapalka, I stopped and helped some Roman Catholic seminarians dig a mass grave for the decomposing bodies still in a school building. That, too, seemed a Christian thing to do. But there were to be other personal encounters as well. At least one has been proven unforgettable. One of our relief workers, G. E. David, brought a young girl to me in the village of Komali. The Christian population of this village had suffered terribly. Most of them were low caste *harijans* and, as such, were the poorest people.

Eleven-year-old Kotamma Taratami was a classic beauty. She had delicate, sensitive features, but her face mirrored the empty sadness in her heart. David told me her name meant "fortress" and as he told me the story of her family, I found myself praying that the strength of the Lord would make her equal to her name.

She would certainly need it.

When the storm struck, Kotamma had been away from the village attending school and staying in a hostel. Komali has no school. The night of the angry winds, her family, along with some 80 other Christians, sought refuge in the small church. It was of cement block construction and was the most substantial building around. In it they felt secure. It had protected them from cyclones before. But these winds were different from those of other years. First of all, they blew stronger than previous ones. The hands on the wind clocks went off the dial when they reached their limit of 120 miles per hour. Secondly, these winds were described as "helter skelter"—they blew erratically in wrenching, reverse gusts.

The masonry walls could not withstand it. Every block was torn from every other block until—quite literally—there was not one stone left standing upon another.

Eighty-four Christians died when the church came apart at the seams. A Hindu correspondent wrote of the tragedy: "Not even the abode of God could shelter these people."

Kotamma's family—her mother, father, older sister and four others—were among those who perished. She was left alone in the world, and my heart ached for her as it did for the two boys also orphaned when the church collapsed.

Kotamma and I walked hand in hand to the little burial ground just outside the village. The red earth was still piled in fresh mounds. Family members had been buried together. Survivors were kneeling at the graves, and their sobs and swaying bodies made it a place of unrelenting sadness.

I wept with them as I moved from grave to grave, praying with and trying to comfort children and widows. At one grave there were two women—an older one and a younger one. Both were widows. The younger one had been a bride of only six months. Her husband had been the son of the older woman, whose husband had also been killed.

As we knelt at the mound of raw earth where Kotamma's parents were buried, I felt her frail body tremble beside me. Suddenly I knew that prayer alone would not be enough. This orphan child needed more than tears, sympathy, and prayer. She needed a home, a family, a future.

And I thought I heard a voice saying to me, "Take care of my lambs."

There can be only one response to that kind of command. When David told me that Kotamma and the two boys would be placed in a World Vision-supported hostel where they could continue their education, I told him that my wife and I would be responsible for the care of the little girl. I knew she was one of those "least ones" in whom our loving Christ incarnates himself and that by ministering to her we would be ministering to him.

What a blessed privilege!

I looked at David and saw that this caring man, too, had tears in his eyes.

"I will take her to my home for the Christmas holidays," he said gently. "My wife and I have only boys —now we shall have a daughter and my sons shall have a sister!"

I think I saw the Good Shepherd smile.

Before I left India, I saw the resilient, strong-willed people of the eastern coast begin to pull together the broken pieces of their lives and start to rebuild their fractured land. Because of the caring response of thousands of people from Western nations, we were able to put $500,000 into the hands of our team in India to assist in relief and rehabilitation.

I think our caring Lord smiled at that, too.

Chapter 9   No Place Left to Run

The Yao tribesman's words echoed in my mind. The man had spoken them softly, almost apologetically.

"All I want out of life is my garden," he had said, "a few pigs, a buffalo so I can work my rice field . . . and an education for my children."

Hardly excessive demands.

He had made the statement sadly. As though he knew his simple needs would never be met.

I knew Winston was feeling the same emotions I felt. Frustration. Anger. Sadness. During the two-hour ride back to Chiang Rai neither of us said much. We didn't need to. I was pretty sure what he was thinking. It doesn't take long to learn a man when you travel with him.

Southeast Asia had come to be as much a part of Winston Weaver's life as it had mine. A member of World Vision's board of directors, this Virginia businessman had put in months of volunteer time supervising the planning and construction of our pediatric hospital in Phnom Penh, Cambodia. The communists took the town as soon as the hospital was finished, so he never got to see it in operation.

Wyn loves the people and the land as much as I do.

A Meo tribeswoman and her baby from Laos are at the end of a long and sorrowful trail as they sit in a refugee camp in northern Thailand. Literally, they are at trail's end.

This survey of the needs of nearly 80,000 refugees from Cambodia and Laos now living in Thailand was as wrenching for him as it was for me. The sights, the sounds, the conversations—they all had combined to reopen the emotional wounds still not completely healed.

Now, driving back from the refugee camp near the Mekong River to Chiang Rai, Thailand's northern-most city, we were remembering those who had been left behind when the communists took over.

And the words of that Yao hill tribesman from Laos disturbed our thoughts. His life's ambition: a garden, some pigs, a buffalo and an education for his children. . . .

But the new politicians in Vientiane are more in-terested in "re-educating" the Yaos than in allowing them to raise pigs. Almost half of the tribe's 11,000 members have fled across the Mekong to Thailand. One tribal leader estimates that 80 percent of those remaining in Laos would like to leave.

For the moment, "leaving" means a one-way trip on a dead-end street into the stifling boredom of a refugee camp. The best part about it, one man tells me, is that "we are away from the communists." When a crowded, fenced, guarded refugee camp can represent freedom, I am suddenly aware of the rela-tive meaning of that word.

Some of the thousands in the camps have spent most of their lives escaping. For the Thai Dam (Black Thai) tribespeople, this is their fifth home in less than one generation. They fought with the French against the Vietminh in their homeland near Dien Bien Phu. Each successive move from North Viet-nam, through Laos, to Thailand has been just one step ahead of the communist expansion in Southeast Asia.

Now they sit quietly in barbed wire camps, a small

retinue of Thai soldiers standing sentry at the gate. The guards are there as much to protect the unarmed refugees from the communist terrorists who prowl the jungle of northern Thailand as they are to keep the refugees inside.

For these homeless strangers, there is no place else to run.

When you ask the refugees what will become of them now, most merely shrug their shoulders. They know they are a political embarrassment and an economic burden to Thailand. But they do not consider going back to be an option. For many, if not for most, it would mean death. At the least it would mean separation from their families by assignment to a "re-education" camp. The thought of this terrifies them because of the thousands who never returned to their villages from such camps.

Their only hope is that Thailand might allow them to remain for an extended period of time or that a third country will allow them to immigrate there. For the educated among them, a new life as immigrants in a developed country would be relatively easy. For the rice farmers, it would be more difficult.

It is also difficult for Thailand to consider giving them permanent residence. Such a solution would create strain and tension with the rural Thais alongside whom the newcomers would live. For the foreseeable future, the refugees would be an economic burden on a government which cannot provide the minimal social services even for its own people.

The dilemma is considerable.

Meanwhile, life goes on at the camp. It has to. The children somehow always manage to play. Young men and women meet, fall in love, and marry. Mothers have babies. Middle-aged couples bury their parents—who carry to their graves faces etched with decades of the struggle for survival.

The camps in northern and eastern Thailand are jammed with Cambodians, Haw, Meo, Yao, and a half-dozen other tribal names. The places where they are located are not exactly household names in the West, either: Chiang Kong, Chiang Saen, Aranyaprathet, Nong Khai.

As we walked through the camps day after day and talked with the refugees, I was once again assaulted with the depressing similarity of the life of refugees around the world.

A line of empty water buckets snaking its way across the dirt courtyard, waiting for the daily delivery of the precious liquid; the look of boredom like thousands of carbon copies on expressionless faces; malnutrition flourishing in the frail bodies of small children—beriberi, scabies, eye diseases.

I had seen it all before. In the nomad camps outside Niamey, Niger. On the India/Bangladesh border when twelve million Bengalis came across like a tidal wave to escape the civil war. In Ethiopia. In Mindanao. And South Vietnam.

You think after a while you will get used to it, that your sensitivities will become numb. But here in northern Thailand I was seeing it again and still the sickening sameness hit me deep in my emotional center.

On the way back to Chiang Rai, I mentally evicted myself from my own home. I reduced my food allowance to the minimum necessary to sustain life, took my children out of school, removed my medicine cabinet . . . and declared myself a refugee. I think I might have, for a brief moment, felt the pain of losing everything. But I couldn't be sure I *really* felt anything, because for me it was only an exercise in mental gymnastics.

For the refugees we had just left it was not a game. It was cruel, stark reality. The kind that strips you of your sense of worth and causes you to question the value of life.

We spent long hours with the leaders in the camp, with small children, with mothers and father. We talked over cups of tea or soft drinks. The theme was always the same: We're glad we no longer have to run, but what are we to do now?

Boredom takes its toll. Too much time to let the mind wander. To think. To remember . . . aging parents left behind . . . sometimes children left behind, with the hope of being reunited later in freedom . . . other familiar faces . . .the memories of childhood.

Aranyaprathet is a Thai village hard against the Cambodian border. Nearby is a refugee camp, bursting at the seams with 3,500 Cambodians. The boundary between the two countries—just a few kilometers down the road—is a steel bridge over a small river. It is easy to spot the exact border demarcation because the Thai half of the bridge is painted white. At midpoint, the bridge is rusty and unpainted.

A few local Thais move freely across the bridge, now and then engaging in barter economy with the Khmer Rouge on the other side. However, our white faces are quickly spotted by the two Khmer Rouge soldiers who sit beneath the solid red communist flag across the short bridge. Although their rifles stay in a relaxed position, their eyes do not leave us as we make our way to the middle, trying to appear as if we are out for a casual stroll.

Somehow it didn't seem right. It was as if I were being kept out of *my* country. I felt deprived, cheated, dispossessed. For five years I had adopted the Cambodian people, and they had adopted me.

Now I was so close and yet a million ideological miles away.

I thought about our friends, the pastors and church

leaders, our earlier evangelistic campaigns. I knew Winston was thinking about our hospital.

It was hard to turn and walk away, but there was nothing we could do for those inside. For now, our ministry must be with those in the camps. They have needs, too. The United Nations has announced that it will make no more monetary appropriations for them. Most of the other private agencies have moved on to other lands and other people. We have told the Thai government that we will stay and help as many of the 80,000 as we can.

Every single one of them has a story to tell if you have the time to listen. What I heard from those at Aranyaprathet was almost more than I could take emotionally. I have no way of knowing if some of the stories were simply rumors, repeated and embellished slightly with each telling. Maybe so. But there were hard facts, too. And personal experiences. There was too much evidence for it all to have been fabricated.

Correspondent H. D. S. Greenway, writing for the *Washington Post* (Feb. 2, 1976), described life in Cambodia today by saying, "Cambodia remains a tightly closed society. . . . The emphasis in Cambodia is on work and more work under the threat of punishment . . . Everybody, including the sick, the old and the children, was forced out into the fields . . . there are still no newspapers . . . modern medicines are in short supply . . . people live on a barter economy."

According to one refugee from a village, the Khmer Rouge threatened that his entire village would be killed if they opposed the regime. "They were told," he said, "that if this happened, the neighboring village would be forced to bury them and they would be forced to bury the neighboring village if they misbehaved."

Perhaps genocide is too broad and prejudicial a

word to use for what is going on in Cambodia today. But no responsible person to whom I spoke—both in and out of the camps—doubts that large segments of the population are being slaughtered or allowed to die.

It is cynical, inhuman, and insane.

The Bangkok Post (March 2, 1976) editorialized: "To be brutally honest, the leaders of the Khmer Republic seem at the present time to be not only totally sadistic to their own people, but to have lost total contact with reality. The sadism, the mass beatings, killings and (forced) labor, have been documented in such great detail recently that even the most ardent leftist can only look at that country with repugnance."

Douang Seak is twenty–two years old. Before April 1975, he was a drafted soldier in the Cambodian Army. He talked without hesitation about life since then under the Khmer Rouge:

"The people in Cambodia today are dying for three reasons: first, starvation. Most people get only two bowls of rice a day—rice and water is all they get. Second, disease is spreading rapidly throughout the entire country, particularly malaria. A lot of dysentery, too. There is almost no medicine left. Medical facilities simply don't exist. Third, anyone who is educated or worked for the former government is put on a list to be killed. It is dangerous to have any education at all."

He told of people being brutally clubbed to death, indicating this, rather than shooting, is the favored method of execution.

I asked Douang Seak if he had seen these horrors with his own eyes. He answered: "I escaped fifteen days ago. I have seen all these things with my own eyes. It is all true."

I felt an uneasy mixture of pain, anger, and frustration. Since I couldn't verbalize my feelings in response, Douang Seak continued: "I was at the end of my rope. I just didn't know what to think. I couldn't believe Cambodians were killing Cambodians like this. My own relatives are still there and I know they might already be dead. But what are we to do?"

He didn't expect an answer from me, nor did he wait for one: "The people in Cambodia still hope that we who have escaped are going to get weapons and return to rescue and deliver them from the Khmer Rouge. My friends all believe they will die if they stay in Cambodia, so they figure it's worth an attempt to revolt against the soldiers. If they decide to try to escape, they'll have two chances—either they will die or they will make it."

Apparently life is reduced to these two basic choices. I didn't have the heart to tell Douang Seak that the world has all but forgotten Cambodia, choosing to let it disappear behind a curtain of silence and isolation, and that if his friends made it they would have to do it all by themselves.

To have told him that would have crushed all hope, and hope is all they have left—hope that a caring world will rise in moral indignation against the inhuman practices of their Khmer Rouge taskmasters. How do you tell such a gentle and trusting people that the United Nations is too busy with South Africa and the Middle East to bother with a mere six million Cambodians?

The society currently run by the Khmer Rouge is primitive in the extreme. There are no more "urban" or "rural" designations—everyone is in the rice paddy. The towns and cities are deserted, the people driven into the forests and fields. The economy is on the barter system. The Cambodian revolution bears no resemblance to classic Marxism. It is a peasant revolution with almost no political sophistication.

Someone at the top of the whole gruesome episode must be smart enough to have a master strategy, but the guards at the bottom were portrayed to me as being, for the most part, illiterate and unfeeling robots. The only exceptions he had seen, one man told me, were among the older Khmer Rouge soldiers who seemed to show some regrets over the killings.

A recent escapee told me that the only medicine available in his area was that left by the Americans. He had been a teacher, but was assigned to be a medical worker—because he could read the instructions on the bottles. His medical supplies had been quickly exhausted, he said, and the people were reduced to using leaves and roots with known medicinal qualities.

I inquired about the children. We had helped so many.

"There are thousands of orphans in Cambodia today," a refugee told me. He had come just three weeks before, alternately trekking and hiding out in the jungle for four days. "They have either been separated from their parents or their parents have been killed. They have no place to go and they must scrounge for food.

"The children are afraid. If they are under six years of age, the Khmer Rouge allows them to stay with their families. Those over six are taken away to work in the fields and to receive a political education."

I asked about his own family.

He had been forced to leave them—his wife and three children. "Why was it necessary for you to run?" I asked. He had learned that his name was on a list for extermination.

But why?

"I had an education and was dangerous to them." It was an answer I was to hear spoken many times.

I later remarked to Don Scott, World Vision's director in Thailand who was also serving as interpreter, about the man's matter-of-fact answers, his composure—in fact, the absence of any outward emotion. I wondered about his sincerity, his truthfulness.

Old Asia-hand Don gave me a cultural insight: "Most Asians don't publicly display their emotions, but that doesn't mean they don't feel deeply inside. That man was emotional, all right. You wouldn't have caught it, but he used words that expressed deep and strong feelings. Often this doesn't come across in translation. Did you notice that he was speaking with clenched fists? You don't see that very often. That simple demonstration spoke volumes about his emotional trauma.

"But, Stan," Don continued, "most of these refugees have accepted their fate and thrown in the towel. They have been through the wringer of life's most shattering experiences. They've lost virtually everything, including their families. Many have just given up. They have simply run out of emotion."

I thought about that a lot. The camps in Thailand are places where people have run out of just about everything—homeland, human dignity, hope.

One Meo leader spoke of the difficulties of maintaining family life in a country run by the Pathet Lao (Laotian Communists): "The Pathet Lao are just ripping our families apart. My wife was taken from me. My children, too. They wouldn't let me see them. Sometimes I got so lonely I would write a letter to myself and sign my wife's name. Sure, I knew it was just pretending.

"I couldn't find them so I had to leave alone. We want our families with us because if we die in the camp in Thailand, at least we will die together. But if we die over there, we die apart. I don't know where I will go. Or what I will do."

He was a sensitive, gentle man. He hurt deeply. There was obvious pain as he spoke of his wife and children. He had no one. No place to go. Nothing to do.

He will continue to just sit there in the camp until someone, somewhere, decides what is going to happen to him. He waits . . . and waits . . . for nothing.

He dreams about his children, his garden, his pigs, and his rice field. He doesn't know if he'll ever find them again—or where.

Because there's no place left to run.

Chapter 10

God's Second Visit to Timor

Almost as soon as I said it, I wondered if I had done the right thing.

It had been spontaneous. Unpremeditated. Spirit-directed, I thought at the time.

But then I began to wonder if I hadn't been simply brash, presumptuous, and foolish.

Here's what had happened. I was leading a Bible study at the 6 A.M. spiritual life seminar on the Indonesian island of Timor. The morning seminars were part of an evangelistic crusade being conducted in the capital city of Kupang by the Rev. Petrus Octavianus and myself at the invitation of the Timorese Evangelical Church and government officials.

We had already seen great blessing—by mid-week the crowds were up to 35,000 a day, thousands were responding to the invitation to receive Christ, scores were surrendering fetishes and charms for burning. God's power was being greatly felt in the meetings.

Our only distress was that it had been our intention to produce an evangelistic film of the crusade for use on television and throughout Indonesia, but thus far the government had refused our request for permits for the film crew. They had been sitting in Jakarta for four days—waiting. Waiting for clearance of

So many thousands responded to the invitation to receive Christ when Petrus Octavianus and I led a crusade on the island of Timor that this Indonesian evangelist had to counsel them en masse.

the equipment through customs. Waiting for first one department and then another to give the necessary permits. On Timor, time was running out as we waited and prayed.

That was how on Thursday morning, during an exposition of Matthew 18 to the more than 500 believers at the spiritual life seminar, I had made my bold —or brash—statement. I had been talking about the astounding potential in a reconciled community of believers. We came to verse 19: "Again I say unto you, that if two of you shall agree on earth as touching any thing that they shall ask, it shall be done for them of my Father which is in heaven." I pointed out that the number of persons was not the key factor in that verse. The critical word was "agree." I told them the number might be two or 500, if they truly agreed.

And then I said something like this: "Either that verse means what it says or else it is so much pious rhetoric. If it doesn't work in life's day-to-day experiences, it isn't worth anything as a beautiful spiritual theory. The only qualification I can put on it is that we agree *in the will of God.*"

I told them of our desire to film the crusade. Of the frustrations and red tape we had experienced. How after searching our own hearts in prayer, Petrus Octavianus and I believed that what we wanted was for God's glory and in his will.

Then I wanted to know how many of them would agree with us to ask and believe God for the arrival of the film team before the end of the crusade. I told them I wanted to see if Jesus was as good as his word. Scores—perhaps a couple of hundred—raised their hands. We sealed our agreement in prayer and I went on with the study.

It wasn't long until I began to wonder if I had led the people in a commitment which might later be faith-shattering. The tempter didn't leave me alone.

All the rest of the week I alternated between "Lord, I believe" and "Help my unbelief."

Through the archaic telephone system in Timor, I tried to monitor the progress in Jakarta, over a thousand miles away. We had a line only two hours a day and it ran under the Straits of Java. Salt water and time had combined to ravage it and make almost every conversation unintelligible.

A few phrases came through, however, "Equipment cleared through customs." On Friday..."Final O.K.... taking last plane to Denpasar" (on the island of Bali, the only point of departure to Kupang, still six hundred miles away.)

Hope began to rise.

On Saturday a call from Bali.

Again, barely intelligible:

"No more flights till Monday!"

Too late.

"Try a charter."

"Will do."

Wait...pray...no, *believe*...*agree*.

Another call. They had managed to charter an old DC-3, but the plane couldn't take the film team plus equipment *plus* enough fuel for the return flight. That last one was the catch. We had to arrange DC-3 fuel on Timor!

Pak Octavianus (Bapak—shortened to Pak—is an Indonesian title of respect) went to the court of last resort, the Governor of Timor. He is a believer... had warmly welcomed the evangelistic team at a reception at his home... had attended almost every crusade meeting, and had chosen to sit on the ground among the people rather than on the platform because, as he said. "I want the eyes of the people to be on God, not on some government official."

Governor El Tari would help us. I knew he would. So he became the source of my confidence and faith.

It was now one o'clock Saturday afternoon. Pak Octavianus went to the governor's home. He was back at the guest house within an hour with sad news. The governor had agreed to do everything within his power to help us. However, fuel for a DC-3 was not in his power. There was only a small amount on the island . . . it belonged to the military and was needed for operations in the war with Portuguese East Timor which raged in the mountains of the island.

The court of last resort had failed! Utterly crushed, I asked the clerk at the guest house to see if telephone central could get Bali so I could relay the disappointing final message.

Then I went to my room. I didn't argue with God. I simply acquiesced—reluctantly, I admit—merely because I no longer had any strength for the struggle. I told God I didn't understand it, but if that's the way he planned it, I would accept it. I said it was up to him to straighten it out with the Timorese Christians who had agreed with me to take him at his word.

I lay down on my narrow bed . . . emotionally spent.

Not ten minutes later, Pak Octavianus burst into my room. While the clerk was trying to get through to Bali, the leader of the film team there had gotten through to us and announced wildly—there was no time for details—that they would be arriving at ten o'clock the next morning. Sunday . . . the last day of the crusade.

But how? How? I tried to figure it out. They must have been able to charter a twin Otter from one of the commercial companies and since it was a small plane, they would bring only a part of the team and some of the equipment.

So I reasoned. But at least we went to the crusade meeting on Saturday with our spirits high. Fifty thousand people jammed the soccer field that day. We announced the good news . . . and told the people to wear their beautiful, colorful national dress the next day.

On Sunday morning I went to the deserted airport about 9:30 and began to watch the skies for a twin Otter on which I was sure they were arriving. The man in the radio tower told me that no such plane was scheduled to arrive and that he had had no radio contact.

I left the tower, a little shaken but undaunted.

In the meantime, an Indonesian military DC-3 had landed and was unloading. I paid no attention until I heard shouts from that direction. It was the entire film team! While I had been watching the skies for a commercial twin Otter, God had sent them with all the equipment on a military plane.

The story they told was that of a miracle. Just about the same time I had found out there was no fuel on the island, the telephone had rung back in the hotel room of the team leader on Bali. A voice had said:

"I understand you wish to go to Kupang."

"Yes, yes!"

"We have a military plane ready to go to Kupang."

"When?"

"When do you want to leave?"

"We'll be at the airport in half an hour."

An officer had overheard a conversation at the Denpasar airport about a film team trying to get to Timor. He had inquired and found out that the name and hotel of the man who had tried to charter a plane. For those who will say, "What an astounding coincidence!" I can only reply with the words of George Müller: "Some people say the amazing things that happen to me are coincidences. Maybe so. All I know is that when I pray the coincidences happen, and when I don't pray, they don't happen."

I know this—that military plane was the only way our team could have gotten to Timor. It was able to fly half-way on Saturday, land at a military base and refuel for the completion of the flight on Sunday morning.

God had literally brought us down to the wire. The film was made and shown on television. It is presently being used as an evangelistic tool in Indonesia with an Indonesian interpretation.

Did that miracle strengthen my faith? I suppose so, although I don't expect the next test of faith to be any easier. Marion Allen, a Christian and Missionary Alliance missionary who went through this test with us, said something which helped me. He said: "I have learned that when God's name is at stake, he will move heaven and earth to protect his name."

I believe that. The whole crusade was an evidence of that. The very fact that I was in Timor at all was something of a miracle. The government in Jakarta hadn't been too happy about the whole thing. For one thing, elections were less than a year away and they didn't want any overt Christian activity putting a further strain on Muslim-Christian relationships. Then, too, the island of Timor—approximately 100 by 300 miles—was still the scene of its own stress. A nasty civil war had been going on for nearly a year in the mountainous border area only 250 miles from Kupang. It was the border which had divided the island into Indonesian Timor and the former Portuguese colony of East Timor.

When the Portuguese left, Indonesia annexed the territory with a population of 600,000, but not without some violence and criticism in the United Nations. Understandably all this had created a sensitivity which made the idea of an outdoor evangelistic crusade less than popular in Jakarta. Permission for the meetings and for my participation as a foreigner came only two days before the campaign was to begin.

Undoubtedly, the most strategic single factor in this approval was the personal appeal to the military authorities by His Excellency, Governor El Tari. He told them: "We need this evangelistic effort to strengthen the spiritual life of our people."

Happily, not a single incident marred the week of meetings.

The vision for the crusade was placed in the heart of the Rev. B. Meroekh while attending the 1974 Lausanne Congress on Evangelization. A senior pastor and former chairman of the synod of the Timorese Evangelical Church, Mr. Meroekh came back and convinced church and government leaders that it was once again God's time for the island of Timor.

He had been one of the leaders of the widely reported Timorese revival of the mid-1960s (See Chapter 4). In speaking of that visitation of the Holy Spirit and the accompanying physical miracles of a decade ago, Pastor Meroekh said the churches were not then prepared to do an adequate job of follow-up and much of the revival results had been sidetracked into erroneous emphases by overzealous workers.

He told me that at the time of the earlier visitation of the Spirit, he had been chairman of the evangelization department of the synod. As such, he was deeply involved in the revival and witnessed many healings. He stated categorically, however: "I know there were no such things as resurrections from the dead."

He went on to say that whereas in the earlier revival, healings were accomplished by those members of the evangelistic teams specially gifted by the Holy Spirit, now they were being experienced by pastors and elders in many churches.

As advisor of the evangelistic teams in the Kupang

area which sprang from the mid-60s revival, Pastor Meroekh had encouraged all the members to be involved in the crusade "so they would be really refreshed and renewed again."

"I believe they are stronger now," he said, "because of the biblical preaching of this crusade which has emphasized the new birth, cleansing from sin, and the victorious power of Christ. It will not be as easy as before for them to fall into pride, jealousy, and sexual sins."

It was amazing to me to see tens of thousands standing for three to four hours, listening to solid Bible teaching, for that's essentially what the crusade sermons were. Both Octavianus and I were led day after day to speak on the themes Pastor Meroekh had mentioned. The Holy Spirit was using the Word in a remarkable way. After the second day, a group came to some members of the crusade committee and told them: "At first we came because we wanted to hear the music, but now God's Word is speaking to us so forcibly that we would just as soon you omit the music and let's spend the whole time in the Scriptures."

Well, we didn't do that because God was using the Spirit-anointed ministry of soloist Gary Moore, guitarist Eddie Karamoy, an anklung orchestra from Surabaya, and a musical group from the Indonesian Bible Institute on the island of Java. Together, the music and the spoken word were making a tremendous spiritual impact.

The audience grew daily until an estimated 50,000 people filled Merdeka (Freedom) Stadium for each of the two closing services. That is all the more amazing when you consider that Kupang has a population of only 60,000! The people came not only from Timor, but from others of the islands forming what is known as the Lower Sunda group—islands with names like

Sumba, Roti, Samau, Alor, Flores. Some of them were 400 miles away. Day after day, fishing boats of all descriptions pushed their way on to the soft coral sand beaches.

Then they made their way to the stadium, which may be a bit too grand a name. It was really a large, open soccer field. Everyone was on the playing field, because there were no "stands" as in sports arenas in the Western world. They either sat on the ground or stood.

The small platform at one end of the field was about the only place which was illuminated. Nine fluorescent tubes lit the platform, but the rest of the field boasted a total of six forty-watt bulbs—scarcely enough to let the preacher see his audience. The meetings started at 4 P.M. while it was still daylight, but usually didn't conclude until 7:30 or 8 o'clock. By then the sun had set in a purple haze through the palm trees—a daily sight still etched in my memory.

The response to the nightly invitation to receive Jesus Christ was overwhelming. Even from the first day it was impossible to do individual counseling since there were only 100 trained counselors. Thus Pak Octavianus counseled thousands *en masse* from the platform. So many were indicating a desire to know Jesus that it soon became impractical to have them come forward. We simply asked for a show of hands—always numbering into the thousands—and then Octavianus spent from thirty minutes to an hour instructing them in basic biblical doctrines.

Evidence of genuine repentance and faith began to show up as scores of people gave up the charms and fetishes which bound them to witchcraft. I was told this is a major problem in the churches. To give up these objects which supposedly possess supernatural power because they came from the witch doctor required great faith and commitment.

Anything—pieces of wood, knives, glass jars with a variety of murky contents, dirty rags—could receive Satanic power if the individual surrendered them to the evil spirits. Soon sacks began to fill up, and the crusade officials planned for a fetish burning on the closing day as a demonstration of the power of God over Satan.

It was my first such experience—and what an experience! As the devices of witchcraft and the occult were put to the torch, the people began singing a chorus of triumph and victory. God had done "exceedingly abundantly above all that we could ask or think." The very atmosphere seemed charged with the presence of God.

Pak Octavianus explained to me: "Witchcraft is one of the major obstacles to evangelism in Asia today. Our people have for centuries lived in touch with the spirit world. With this kind of control over much of Asian culture, Satanism exerts great influence in the lives of the people. It is a great spiritual event when people indicate publicly a break with the powers of darkness."

The liberating power of Christ showed on the beaming tan faces as they sang and clapped their hands. As I watched the flames from the burning fetishes leap heavenward, pushing back the closing Timorese darkness, I had the distinct feeling that God was visiting Timor again.

Again, as at the cross, Satan's impotence was being put on open display.

"Hallelujah! puji Tuhan!" the people sang.

My heart echoed, "Hallelujah! Praise the Lord!"

Chapter 11 The People Behind the Wire

Somewhere in Salisbury a disc jockey cued up "O Little Town of Bethlehem" on the turntable, dropped the needle, and sent the radio signal out into the December air.

But at Keep 13, some seventy miles to the north, no one seemed to notice the strains of the carol— picked up and piped out from the central administrative building—as they came through the loudspeakers and spilled out over the huts and shacks.

The people "behind the wire" in Rhodesia are too numb to notice much of anything. Caught in the middle of the conflict which will ultimately bring black majority rule to their southern African country, the 4,000 people in Keep 13 appeared suspended in time and space.

I've been in many refugee and resettlement camps all over the world, but the mood inside this one felt different. I can best describe it as eerie and ominous. The children seemed listless—I didn't see a single one playing, a phenomenon I have rarely seen in even the most desperate situation. One woman dug away with mechanical motions at the hard ground around her little plot of yams. Another plaited her hair as she sat in the doorway of her hut with two of her children.

The mind and soul-deadening inactivity of life in the "protected villages" of Rhodesia hardly seems a fair trade for the freedom of village life to this Shona woman and her children.

Several teenagers sat silently on a pile of logs.

The song from Salisbury added a note of incongruity to the scene: it was nearly Christmas, but that would make little or no difference to most of the people in Keep 13 or the hundreds of other "keeps" throughout the countryside. For them, there hasn't been a Christmas or any other holiday worth celebrating since 1974.

That was the year they were put "behind the wire."

That's what the Rhodesian blacks call it. The white government says the blacks are put in the "protected villages" to give them security against terrorist raids. On the maps of the Ministry of Interior, the villages are designated as "keeps," and each one is given a number. Government officials declined to give me the total number of blacks who have been uprooted, but did admit that a "fair number of the population" have been placed in this semi-detention.

With a black population of about 5.9 million in Rhodesia, my estimate is that several hundred thousand people, mostly in the border areas, have been affected by these government efforts to contain the guerilla war.

The government claim of security is partly true. That's one of the problems in Rhodesia today—virtually everything you hear is *partly* true. It has nothing to do with dishonesty, but rather with perspective. It is terribly difficult for those emotionally involved with the issues of independence and white control vs. black majority rule to be totally objective.

Take the keeps, for example. To the government, they are necessary as part of the effort to deny local support to the guerrillas, as well as to protect the villagers from intimidation by the terrorists. On this basis, they seem fully justified to those who conceived them.

But for those affected, it has been total trauma.

They have been removed from tribal and family lands where they have lived for generations. At first it was done haphazardly, with haste and without warning. Trucks came to the villages, loaded the people and their belongings on and then dumped them behind the wire onto a bare spot of ground fifty feet square. They suffered much hardship until they could build their own huts to protect them from the rain and elements.

Their bodies suffered from hunger and cold. Their spirits suffered from disorientation and the loss of dignity. Few deny that there was some brutality and abuse.

Later the government took more care when it moved the people, but nothing could soften the shock of the break-up of familial and social patterns or compensate for the loss of freedom.

For centuries the tribal peoples of Rhodesia have lived by the extended family concept. All close relatives live in a compound called a *kraal*. The average *kraal* may have ten or more huts. The parents live in one, cooking is done in another, the grandparents may have two, the boys have a hut and so do the girls, while other older relatives may each have one.

The farming land is immediately adjacent to the *kraal*. The goats and cattle graze nearby.

The social order is well established. What the life style may lack in affluence, it makes up for in family solidarity.

Behind the high-security fence, life is topsy-turvy. Families are crowded in on top of each other. The fields are five to ten miles away, yet each family is expected to grow its own food. The animals cannot be tended.

What they do have behind the wire is water, normally a scarce commodity. It may be pumped from the nearest muddy river, but it is piped to several outlets within the camp. But taken on balance, one would have to say that the convenience of water doesn't make up for the inconvenience of trying to farm the land so far away.

There is electricity, too, although it is not for individual use, but to power the big fluorescent street lights—all turned outward around the camp perimeter to deter a night terrorist attack.

I walked around the camp with the camp director and with Mr. Kazunga, the head of one of the family *kraals* in Keep 13. The 23-year-old director—a likeable chap and the only white among the 4,000 blacks —pointed out to me several times that Mr. Kazunga was a chronic complainer.

My own observation was that Mr. Kazunga had quite a bit to complain about, although I discovered that not everyone in the camp shared his views. Yet, even in talking with the people, I had the feeling that most of the time I was not getting their true or deepest feelings. Sometimes they spoke vaguely or gave contradictory views in the same conversation.

They have learned to be careful and evasive because they don't know who is going to win. Since there are terrorist sympathizers as well as government employees in the camp, they wisely don't want to be on record with any definitive statements for which they may later have to answer.

But Mr. Kazunga was different. Quietly bitter about the whole experience, he didn't seem to care.

He had come home early from the fields that day because he was too weak to work. The people are forbidden to take any food outside the camp for fear they will give it to the guerrillas who operate in the area. For some the fear is not unfounded: Keep 13 is in what is called a "hot spot." Less than a month after I was there, five Roman Catholic missionaries were killed not many miles from Keep 13.

As Mr. Kazunga told me his story, I began to get some insights into the problems faced by nearly all the people. In his *kraal* there are eleven people. They have been in the protected village over two years.

During that time he has walked almost every day to his fields and gardens six miles away.

That made a twelve–mile round trip. Normally, he would have been in his fields at sunup, but all the people behind the wire are under curfew from 6 P.M. to 6 A.M. Most days they cannot be in their fields before 9 or 10 o'clock because it takes two to three hours to check out of the single gate through which everyone must pass, plus another hour or more to walk to the fields.

In my mind I went over the simple logistics of trying to clear up to 2,000 people in and out of a single gate twice a day. Each person's name is on a large board with a matchstick in a hole beside it. The match must be removed when the person leaves the camp and replaced when he returns. Even allowing just five seconds for each transaction, only 720 people can be cleared in an hour.

Thus many of the people can't be in their fields until the sun is already high, and they must leave again by midafternoon to get back through the gate before curfew. This means they have to work in the heat of the day with no food.

I turned and looked at the young camp director who had been listening to our conversation. He was immediately defensive: "What can I do? We don't have enough money to hire guards to staff another gate. It isn't my fault."

He was right and I didn't blame him. But it was an injustice—and it had to be *someone's* fault.

Mr. Kazunga was caught in the middle. In fact, that's what some people call the people behind the wire—"the people in the middle." They are trapped

between guerrilla fighters determined to force immediate black rule and an equally determined white
government which has finally (maybe too late) agreed
to black majority rule at some time in the future,
after an orderly changeover.

In the vise between the white "sometime" and the
black "now," millions of little people are having the
life and soul squeezed out of them—the white farmer
on his homestead as well as the black farmer in the
government keeps. The terrorists terrorize and
slaughter both.

Shortly after I left Rhodesia, one of the keeps was
attacked by guerrillas. Who knows why? It might
have been retaliation for cooperation with the government, real or imagined. Or it may have been just
another part of terrorist tactics. For whatever reason,
the people were routed out of their huts which were
then burned to the ground.

When a relief team got there, nothing was left but
ashes and the clothes on the victims' backs. Many
children were literally naked. Yet when the team offered assistance, it was stolidly and persistently refused. Again, who knows why? Maybe it was resentment over years of discrimination and mistreatment.
Perhaps a fierce independence. Or fear of further
reprisals from the guerrillas.

One relief official unwisely tried to go around the
resisting parents and offered the goods to the children. A boy of about ten stood up and said: "We do
not want any of your gifts. You can take them away.
We only want to go back to our homes in the bush."

The guerillas—either called "freedom fighters" or
"terrorists," depending on whether you are white or
black—operate mostly from the safety of Rhodesia's
neighbors, principally Mozambique, where they are
given support by the Marxist government. However,
a great deal of support also comes from non-Marxist

African nationalists in neighboring Zambia and Botswana.

There is no problem in finding recruits. A very sophisticated black Rhodesian woman who runs a social service agency told me about her nephew who had insisted on taking her to the airport when she made a recent trip to South Africa. In a quiet corner of the waiting lounge he told her why he wanted to see her off—he would be gone when she got back and he didn't want to tell his parents.

He would just disappear "into the bush" and emerge sometime later as a trained and armed guerrilla. Her eyes searched his face for a reason. "It is the only way," is all he could tell her.

As she told me the story, tears came to her eyes.

"That was over a year ago and we have heard nothing from him. He can't write to us. But every time I read that a certain number of terrorists have been killed, I wonder if he was one of them," she said.

Only the names of white soldiers killed in battle are carried in the Rhodesian press, so the family is likely to wonder for a long time.

The freedom forces themselves are divided into at least four factions, as black leaders vie for power in the new government, whenever it comes. Many times the villagers are caught between their own fighting factions.

After talking with numerous leaders in the country, both black and white, I am convinced that a large majority of Rhodesia's blacks support Bishop Abel Muzorewa of the Methodist Church, probably the most moderate of the nationalist leaders. At least, he was until the Rev. Ndabaningi Sithole, another Methodist clergyman, renounced terrorism and was permitted by Prime Minister Ian Smith to return to Rhodesia in mid-1977 after several years of exile in London.

141

Now it is hoped by many that those two moderates will join forces to provide a strong nucleus around which those who want black rule without violence can rally.

In an interview, Bishop Muzorewa said: "The inalienable rights treasured in so-called Western democracies are flagrantly denied the black people of southern Africa. The unliberated black people of southern Africa want to achieve what the American people achieved in 1776—self-determination, that independence which liberates politically those inalienable rights."

The diminutive cleric said that the Church in Rhodesia has "sown the seeds of liberation in the land the nationalists call Zimbabwe. Credit can and should be given to the church and its mission—not to the communists—for what is now at the heart of evolution and revolution in southern Africa."

He pointed out that 90 percent of the leaders of the now black-controlled nations south of the Sahara are "products of the church" through mission schools and contact with missionaries in their formative years.

Christianity was brought to Rhodesia by Portuguese Roman Catholic Jesuits in the mid-seventeenth century. The first known Protestant missionary was Robert Moffat who, with a group from the London Missionary Society, established a mission station in 1859.

About one-fourth of Rhodesia's population is Christian, and about one-half is Christo–pagan. Tribal religions—primarily animism—account for the remaining one-fourth of the populace. The high percentage of Christo-pagan syncretists is the legacy of some early mission efforts and is a serious problem.

During the last decade strict segregationist government policies have interfered with the work of churches and missions. Although some restrictions are being slowly relaxed, multiracial ministries have been prohibited for churches, schools, hospitals, and all other religious and social welfare services. Not a few churches have been the subject of interference and harrassment.

Even in the face of this considerable political unrest, however, the status of Christianity has improved markedly. The Protestant community has doubled in the last decade and the Catholic community has remained fairly stable. Protestants now number in excess of one million, which includes some 200,000 members belonging to over 70 independent churches. Roman Catholics form a community in excess of 550,000. Because of their heavy involvement in the struggle for majority rule, many whites perceive the black Christian community to be a seedbed of revolutionary action and dissent.

Says Bishop Muzorewa: "We're not against white skins; we're against oppression."

He believes those who have done the most for change are the women's prayer groups that meet at dawn every Friday and Sunday in the churches. They pray for their sons and for the sons of their white friends who are out in the bush hunting each other. It is undoubtedly prayer in one of its most agonizing forms.

I left Rhodesia just five days before Christmas. Once again I thought of the music I had heard over the loudspeakers in Keep 13: " . . . the hopes and fears of all the years are met in thee tonight." When Phillips Brooks wrote the hymn in 1868, he meant the words for Bethlehem.

They could as easily apply to Keep 13 and all Rhodesia as the struggle goes on.

Chapter 12 God Is Still in Control

■ really didn't want to go back.

It had been just four weeks since I was in Phnom Penh. What more could I do? Or say?

Physically, I was utterly weary—bone-weary, the old folks in my home state of Mississippi used to call it. The few days at home really hadn't been *at home*. They rarely ever are. There had been trips. Speaking engagements. And the last two chapters of a book— already past the deadline—to be finished.

Then there was a solid week of filming to be completed. The last scene wasn't shot until 10 o'clock Friday night, at the end of a fourteen–hour day. I was savoring the thought of a change of pace—maybe a few days of rest.

But by Monday morning what had started as a nagging thought had turned into a deep conviction— go back to Southeast Asia! I was tempted to argue the issue with God, but I have long since learned to obey an impulse when I can't shake it off.

This one wouldn't shake.

The stories out of Cambodia and South Vietnam in the spring of 1975 were grim. Calls and cables from our teams there told of a rapidly deteriorating situation. Staggering numbers of refugees. Death and hun-

High over Cambodia in our little chartered Convair 220, we fed and diapered our precious cargo which had been snatched from certain death. The bamboo baskets made me think of Moses.

ger everywhere. Children in desperate need. Staff
working day and night. Supplies running out. Time
running out, too.

All this raised burning questions. Could we find
more critically needed supplies? Could we raise
money for an airlift if supplies were available? What
about our schools in the occupied areas? What infor-
mation could we gather out of the confusion to share
with our sponsors who were concerned about their
children? What should we do with the orphans for
whom we were responsible?

What about the future of our national staff? Which
foreign staff members should be evacuated now?
Who should stay and for how long? How long would
be too long? They want to stay as long as possible,
but who is wise enough to guess the last day?

One more consultation—with my wife. We pray.
She is concerned, but willing that I go if it is necessary. She has never, in thirty years, been unwilling.

Now to tie the loose ends. That meant burning the
midnight oil—literally—to get the book manuscript
to the publisher. It also involved many meetings with
my teammate in World Vision, Ted Engstrom, to set
up two task forces—one to implement "Operation
Lovelift" to get supplies to the field and the other to
handle the orphans whose evacuation to the United
States and Australia had already been anticipated.

Then lift-off on Pan-Am 001 for Bangkok—less
than seventy-two hours after the decision to go.

It was less a lift-off, however, than it was a plung-
ing into a maelstrom of headlines and hourly marvels
from which I emerged two weeks later shaken, exhausted, tearful, relieved, sad, proud, dismayed,
warmed—and with my faith vastly strengthened in a
sovereign God who is still in control of events in
Southeast Asia.

My time there became a saga of faith and miracles

in my mind, and even now as I replay the kaleidoscope of events of those two weeks, some of the scenes and faces freeze-frame on my heart. They won't go away—not that I really want them to. Many of them are painful, but they are also very personal and precious.

One face I can't forget is that of a frightened baby, seen through a crack in the door of the rest room at the back of our little chartered Convair 220 as we were ready to take off from the Saigon airport. We had arrived the day before from Bangkok, after dropping off five tons of milk powder in Phnom Penh, for consultations with director Don Scott and his staff.

Since all commercial flights between Bangkok, Phnom Penh, and Saigon had been suspended, we had looked for an available charter plane. Finally, a shipping company in Bangkok had found us the little twin-engine Convair which was owned and piloted by Bill Taylor, a soldier of fortune who had orbited around Asia for so long he reminded me of some character out of one of the adventure strips—*Terry and the Pirates* or *Steve Canyon*. However, it was his skill and daring that got us into and out of airports that were insecure at best and under regular rocket attack at worst.

While my colleagues and I had spent most of the night deciding evacuation strategy with Don Scott, our plane had been parked in a remote corner of Tansohnhut airport. When we were ready to take off the next afternoon, my son, Eric—who had given up his college spring break to photograph the entire mission—heard a baby cry. I was puzzled and alarmed. In addition to the crew of three, there were only four others on the plane—all adults.

I checked the rest room. Locked from the inside! I pushed hard at the top of the door and it gave enough to reveal the face of a terrified baby, with someone's hand over its mouth. I banged. No response.

Sure that Bill Taylor was trying to pull a fast one, I raced to the cockpit and angrily confronted him. I knew if immigration authorities decided to check the plane before we could take off, the plane would be confiscated and we'd all wind up, not *in,* but *under,* the Saigon jail.

I shouted at him, "This plane doesn't leave the ground until you tell me what's going on and who is in the rest room!"

He kept protesting his ignorance and innocence—and I kept pointing to the rear of the plane where the evidence was.

Finally, the American co-pilot, who had signed on in Bangkok, told us both he was responsible for the stowaways. It was true the pilot had no knowledge of it. Now Bill was as angry as I was. The story came out. There were five stowaways—two Vietnamese women and their three children. One was the wife of the co-pilot and two of the children were his. He showed me their passports. The other woman and baby belonged to another pilot in Bangkok. It had been impossible for them to break through the Vietnamese red tape and get permits to leave the country and join their husbands.

The co-pilot had smuggled them past the airport guards and onto the plane the previous night. Before we came aboard, he had put them into the tiny aft baggage compartment which could be reached through a trap door in the rest room.

He apologized. It was an act of desperation.

What to do? What to do! Only seconds to decide. I remembered the chaos of the evacuation of Danang a few days earlier. I knew there was no way I could dump them back onto the airstrip and still live with myself.

They could stay! That decision, having been made, necessitated the quickest takeoff possible before the plane was checked.

Minutes later when we were airborne, I went back to the rest room, jimmied open the locked door, removed the panel which gave access to the storage compartment in the tail, and brought out five frightened, pathetic human beings. They were drenched with sweat and near collapse. The temperature in their little hideaway had soared to 115 degrees during the day.

After taking off from Tansohnhut, we had to fly a dogleg course to pick up the relatively safe corridor marked by the Mekong River for the flight out of South Vietnam, across Cambodia, and into Thailand. As the co-pilot carefully threaded the plane between the known surface-to-air missile sites, I was relieved that he knew the Mekong Delta like the back of his hand.

Bringing out his wife and babies seemed to be a small price to pay for his lifesaving expertise. As I watched the little ones playing on the floor of the cabin (we had stripped out the seats to make room for cargo), I realized that this, too, was precious cargo —even though it wasn't in our plans or on our passenger manifest.

That thought about the passenger manifest, however, reminded me that we were headed for one more piece of trouble as soon as we landed in Bangkok. Thai immigration authorities were certain to take a dim view of the fact that the women and children had no visas. When we landed, I didn't hang around to see how Bill and his co-pilot handled that one. I was quite sure their previous experiences made them well qualified to make the "necessary arrangements."

Just two days before, we had flown equally precious cargo—twenty-one tiny orphans—from Phnom Penh to Bangkok in the first airlift of homeless children from Cambodia. They all had been abandoned at World Vision's nutrition centers.

It was a mission of mercy we nearly had to scrub at the last minute. Because of interminable delays in getting official clearances in Bangkok (one customs official couldn't understand why a chartered aircraft would be carrying fourteen boxes of disposable diapers!), we were half-an-hour beyond the 4:30 P.M. landing time limit at Pochentong airport, about four miles from downtown Phnom Penh. It was a dangerous hour to land—about the time when the constant rocket attacks were stepped up.

The Bangkok/Phnom Penh sector was a two-hour flight in our small craft—plenty of time to reflect on the mission itself and assess the people sprawled on the floor of the seatless cabin.

There were members of our medical team who had left the same airport to which they were returning just a few days earlier in an official evacuation. Leader of the team was Dr. Penelope Key, a British doctor, and a brave and dedicated servant of Christ. We were bringing out a few of the tens of thousands of children they had loved and cared for over the past eighteen months, and there was no way they were going to stay behind.

On the plane was quiet, hard-working Graeme Irvine, an Australian who had left his homeland to become director of World Vision's division of international relations. There was Al Gjerde, another colleague, who had stayed in Phnom Penh under fire to supervise construction of our seventy-bed pediatric hospital. Ralph Sanford, a writer, was also along.

We had some assorted hitch hikers. With commercial flights canceled, news media people from all over the world were stuck in Bangkok, searching for ways to get to the center of action and report the fall of Phnom Penh. As soon as word got around among the journalistic fraternity, I was deluged with telephone calls.

I promised only a one-way trip for any who were interested. Some were. On board was a Swedish television crew, fortifying their courage with alcohol during the entire flight. An ABC television cameraman also opted to go.

So did Sarah Webb Barrell, correspondent for the *New York Daily News.* Because of the uncertain situation it bothered me to think about leaving her at the airport in Phnom Penh.

We talked about Christian hope and eternal life. She was not a believer. Before we landed, I said to her:

"Sarah, I don't know what you'll find in Phnom Penh. It's extremely dangerous. You may not be able to get out. In any event, I want to give you a survival kit. Please keep it with you. Don't forget it. It isn't guaranteed to save your life, but it's guaranteed to give you eternal life."

She was intrigued.

"You can use it anywhere," I went on. "The kit is just seven simple words: 'God, be merciful to me, a sinner.' It's your eternal survival kit."

Sarah stayed in Phnom Penh and was evacuated just a couple of days later with U.S. embassy personnel.

Finally, there was my nineteen-year-old son, Eric. We had been together on similar missions before, but none so obviously dangerous. When our 5:00 A.M. wake-up call came through from the hotel operator that morning in Bangkok, we both lay in the bed for a few moments.

It was a time to think. The long day before us held many unknown events. We knew we might die. There was no reason to be maudlin or emotional about it. It was just a fact to be faced.

I spoke to him quietly:

"Son, we both know we may not be back in this

hotel bed tonight. I just want to know for sure that if this is our last day together on earth, we'll be together in heaven. Are you sure of your relationship with God through Christ?"

He smiled at me. "Don't worry, dad. Everything's all right."

My eyes were misty. I think his were, too. We had prayer together.

Now it was just about twelve hours later. As Taylor banked the plane for our landing approach, a pall of black smoke rose high in the air from a napalm storage dump hit by a rocket. The wheels touched the runway. Now things must happen fast. Quick turnaround and fast taxi to the apron. Five anxious minutes when the door jams. Finally, it releases under a hammer blow, and the ramp drops.

Flak jackets and helmets are thrust at us. Rockets are hitting about every fifteen minutes.

The babies are waiting in vans off the strip, but before loading our human cargo we had to unload supplies for our Cambodian medical teams—five tons which had arrived in Bangkok on a Flying Tiger cargoliner the previous night as part of Operation Lovelift.

Working like stevedores, we get the milk powder and vitamins off in record time.

Then three vans with the babies come onto the field. A hundred feet separate each van in the event that a rocket finds a target. Loving hands quickly transfer the woven bamboo baskets, each bearing a precious life. I think of Moses, but the present scene strikes me as being slightly incongruous. I smile inside.

The wife and three small children of our Cambodian deputy director, Minh Tien Voan, are at the airport ready to come with us, but they need one more immigration stamp. No time. Voan says don't wait and jeopardize the babies. His family will come some other time.

Although we both know there might not be any other time, I agree with him. The babies come first.

Ramp up.

Door secure.

Start the left engine. The prop turns sluggishly, but it doesn't start.

Start! Start!

It only groans.

Three minutes.

Four minutes.

Voan races across the strip, waving documents in his hand. We lower the ramp. He's gotten the final stamp for his wife's passport!

They and the children are bundled aboard.

The engine starts!

Thank you, Lord. Even the delays are a part of your timing.

Elapsed time from touchdown to takeoff—fifty minutes.

Now we're 8,000 feet over Cambodia. Below, a war rages. Up here we are changing diapers, mixing formula, rocking, holding, cuddling, feeding two babies at a time, mixing vitamin C orange drink for those old enough to drink from cups.

Two hours later in Bangkok, Thai immigration and U.S. embassy officials expedite our clearance into the arms of waiting staff and friends. Charles and Sue Morton are there. This marvelous American couple, business residents of this Asian city, have opened their home to these waifs of war as a temporary stopover on their way to adoptive homes in the U.S. The expatriate community in Bangkok pours out love and care on these tiny victims.

The babies rest.

As we took off from Pochentong airport for the last time, I saw the red tile roof of our World Vision pediatric hospital. It had been scheduled to open the previous week. Everything was ready. Even the surgical instruments had been laid out in the operating rooms.

I am sorry we weren't able to turn it over to the medical staff of the Christian and Missionary Alliance who would have operated it, but I am not sorry we built it even in the face of political uncertainty. Christians invested $400,000 in that facility, and to one without faith it looks like a terrible waste. We didn't get to use it even one day.

But there is no waste with anything invested for the Lord. In the early days when we were deciding about starting the hospital, none of the human signs looked promising. But in prayer, the Lord directed me to Ecclesiastes 11. The early verses speak of risk. In verse 1 we are told: "Cast thy bread upon the waters: for thou shalt find it after many days."

Verse 4 in the Living Bible is the one the Lord used to speak to me directly: "If you wait for perfect conditions, you will never get anything done." The King James version is equally stimulating: "He that observeth the wind shall not sow; and he that regardeth the clouds shall not reap."

I am convinced that yet God will reward the faith and daring of his people for investing money when there was no guarantee of success. Down in my soul I can only say that I feel the real saga of Cambodia may be just beginning.

One of the precious images permanently fixed on my heart is the face of our man—no, God's man— Minh Tien Voan, who elected to stay in his native land and minister in the name of Christ rather than choose the safety of an evacuation.

I tried to convince him otherwise. He turned down all my offers to leave the country. He had numerous chances to evacuate; the last one was an offer by the U.S. embassy to put him on one of the military helicopters which lifted out all remaining foreign personnel and many members of the Khmer government. Kindly but firmly, Voan declined it—just as he had declined my attempts to reassign him to a safe country.

When we could no longer take our chartered plane to Phnom Penh, I talked with Voan by shortwave radio from Bangkok. The day before Phnom Penh fell to the Khmer Rouge, our director-in-exile, Carl Harris, talked to him once again by radio. Voan was overcome with joy. His mother, three sisters and a brother-in-law, had all received Christ as Savior. He was still praying for his father, a Buddhist.

As of today, there has been no further word from him, but I know the Good Shepherd is watching over his sheep. In the meantime, we are watching over his wife and three children whom the Lord miraculously delivered on our last trip.

I can still see Voan's round face, beaming but serious under his helmet, as we went over future plans behind the sandbags of a bunker at the airport, while a rocket exploded a few hundred yards away.

He knew he was in the will of God.

God, be with him.

Be with all those in Southeast Asia whom you have chosen—and who have chosen you.

I know you are still in control.